Buying a Manufactured Home

MHI photo

Buying a Manufactured Home

Home

How to Get the Most Bang for Your Buck in Today's Housing Market

Third, revised,
updated, and
expanded edition
2021 printing

Kevin Burnside
& Robert Bentley

Home Resources Books
are published by
Van der Plas Publications / Cycle Publishing
San Francisco

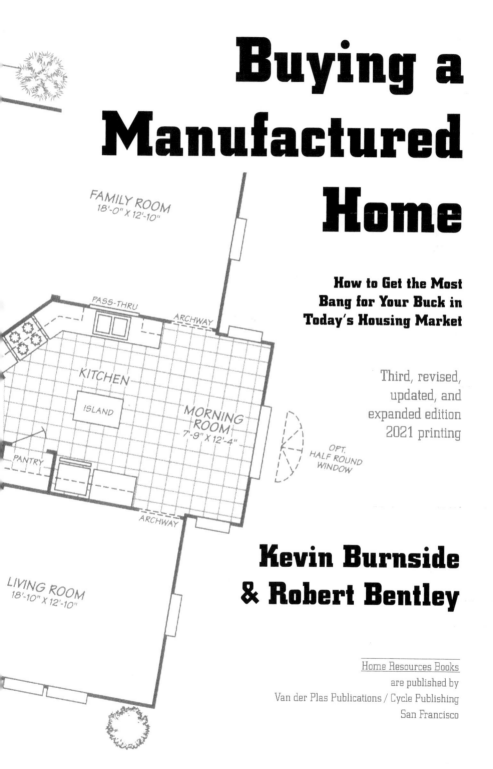

FAMILY ROOM
18'-0" X 12'-10"

PASS-THRU

ARCHWAY

KITCHEN

ISLAND

MORNING
ROOM
7'-9" X 12'-4"

OPT.
HALF ROUND
WINDOW

PANTRY

ARCHWAY

LIVING ROOM
18'-10" X 12'-10"

Third, revised, updated, and expanded edition, 2009
Second printing of this edition, with updates and corrections, 2021

Printed in the USA

Published by:
Van der Plas Publications / Cycle Publishing
1282 7th Avenue
San Francisco, CA 94122, USA
E-mail: rvdp@cyclepublishing.com
Website: http://www.cyclepublishing.com

Distributed to the U.S. book trade by:
Independent Publishers Group, Chicago, IL

Cover design:
Kent Lytle, Lytle Design, Alameda, CA
Cover photographs courtesy Wick Building Systems, Inc., Marshfield, WI
Other illustrations by the authors or as credited

Publisher's Cataloging-in-Publication Data
Burnside, Kevin & Robert Bentley. Buying a Manufactured Home: How to Get
the Most Bang for Your Buck in Today's Housing Market. Third, revised,
updated, and expanded edition
I. Title: How to Get the Most Bang for Your Buck in Today's Housing Market
II Authorship: Bentley, Robert, coauthor
Bibliography: p. cm. Includes index
1. House buying—manuals and handbooks. 2. Manufactured homes & housing.
3. Mobile homes. 3. Modular Housing.
ISBN 978-1-892495-58-7
Library of Congress Control No. 2008939699

To Eloise Dielman, for her time, effort, and hard work.
Thank you!

About the Authors

Kevin Burnside, who grew up in a "mobile home" himself, first became interested in modern manufactured home issues in 1991, while working in real estate. He soon became the top producing salesman for one of the largest Fleetwood dealers in the country, and went on to become sales coordinator for a nationwide manufacturer.

His accomplishments include setting up a customer-friendly sales process along with financial advise and behavior-style training.

His experience affords him keen insights into all aspects of manufactured housing, including selection, contract negotiation, financing, and set-up. Kevin lives with his family in Portland, Oregon.

Robert Bentley is a California-based technical writer and editor with many years of experience in the field. His contributions to this edition of the book can be found primarily in Chapters 3, 10, and 14. In addition, he was responsible for bringing the text up to date with the current state of the art in manufactured home construction and design, site development, and interior design trends.

Table of Contents

1
Introduction

MANUFACTURED HOUSING is becoming an ever-more promising solution to America's housing crisis, especially with the drastic price increases for new and existing homes in the wake of the Covid pandemic. As it is, more than 28 million people in the U.S., or 8% of the population, live in manufactured homes, and in these times of housing turmoil, that share is likely to increase. These modern factory-built houses are a far cry from the trailer homes of yore.

The German architect Walter Gropius was amongst the first to propose factory-built housing, as early as 1910. Nearly twenty years later he brought his idea to the United States, but financial problems, labor

Fig. 1.1. This 2-story home shows how attractive a modern manufactured home can look. Of course, most are still single-story structures.

MHI photo

9

union resistance, and building codes thwarted his attempts. After World War II, however, his dream came true—to an extent. He did not quite see oversized loads being towed on the highways (his plans looked more like panelized construction, shipping individual walls). His dream was further distorted by those wanting to circumvent building codes, and by work rules and resistance from vested interests. The manufactured home industry has responded to a fundamental social need, affordable housing, by marketing a commodity.

Fortunately, today's manufactured homes are far better than the "mobile homes" of the early days. But, because the industry is a business that markets a commodity, you must realize that its interests are not always the same as yours. As with choosing and buying any other product, the burden is on you, the buyer, to assure you're getting the product and quality you want at a price you can afford.

The most important thing to keep in mind throughout the entire process is that it's a negotiating process. At every stage, you will be dealing with salespeople, and with very few exceptions, they will see their job as making the highest possible commission for themselves and the most profit for their employers. That's not unreasonable from their point of view, but it will be your job to promote the other side: getting the most while paying the least.

The purpose of this book is to help you arm yourself with knowledge, so you can put yourself in charge of the home-buying process. This way you won't be "eaten alive" by greedy salespeople and dealers, loan

MHI photo

Fig. 1.2. Interior of a modern high-end manufactured home. We'd say it looks quite nice—if not for that shallow sloping ceiling. It should be either flat, stepped, or much steeper.

brokers, and uncaring contractors. Yes, you can get a fair deal from good manufacturers, reputable dealerships, and honest sales people. But the best way to find those is to be well informed about the entire process and to be as knowledgeable as you can about every aspect of it.

Over the years we've worked in the industry, we've found that not only has the quality and price of manufactured homes gone up considerably, but also that the typical buyer has become more sophisticated.

Table 0.1. U.S. Home sales development since 2003
Manufactured home shipments and single-family housing starts and homes sold

Year	Manufactured home shipments	New home starts	Man. homes as % of total	New single fam. homes sold	Man. homes as % of all
2003	130,937	1,499,100	8.0%	1,088,000	10.7%
2004	130,802	1,610,500	7.5%	1,203,000	9.8%
2005	146,744	1,715,800	7.9%	1,283,000	10.3%
2006	117,510	1,465,300	7.4%	1.052,000	10.0%
2007	95,769	1,046,100	8.4%	766,000	11.0%
2008	81,889	622,100	11.6%	503,000	14.0%
2009	49,789	445,000	10.1%	374,000	11.7%
2010	50,046	488,500	9.3%	322,000	13.5%
2011	51,606	132,300	10.7%	305,000	14.5%
2012	54,891	535,300	9.3%	369.000	12.9%
2013	60,210	617,700	8.9%	429,000	12.3%
2014	64,344	641,000	9.1%	440,000	12.8%
2015	70,519	714,600	9.0%	503,000	12.3%
2016	81,169	780,900	9.4%	563,000	12.6%
2017	92,891	858,900	9.9%	613,000	13.2%
2018	96,540	824,900	10.5%	584,000	14.2%
2019	94,633	887,700	9.6%	682,000	12.2%
2020	94,401	991,100	8.7%	810,000	10.4%

Notes:

"New single family home starts" are new site-built plus manufactured homes that were constructed during the year.

"New single family homes sold" are those site-built plus manufactured homes that actually sold during the year.

Not shown here was the earlier period, with peak figures for the 1994–1997 years, followed by a steady decline to about 1/3 of those peak figures.

For up-to-date statistics on the industry, visit http://www.manufacturedhousing.org.

Although the largest segment of the manufactured home buyers market is still the less affluent and elderly, there are now also homes that appeal to the more affluent and younger sectors of the population—at a price, of course.

As site-built homes continue to increase in cost, more well-to-do folks are taking notice of factory-built homes due to their vast improvement in design, construction, and furbishing. Fifty or so years ago, "mobile homes," or "trailers," were an affordable means of shelter for people with meager to modest incomes. Today, people with meager to modest incomes still have this opportunity to buy a home, but some of the industry's offerings are substantial enough to appeal to those who could afford a conventionally built house. What they are getting is more square feet for the money spent and a quicker turnaround time.

Our intention with this book is to help you save time and money, while giving you peace of mind. Buying a home, whether manufactured or site-built, can be a taxing project. It's probably the single largest purchase you will make in your life. This book will help you deal with the process.

Although we have some harsh words for some of the practices that are only too common in this business, we are not out to "get" the indus-

Fig. 1.3. The low end of today's manufactured housing market, this is a two-bedroom single-wide. Note how even such a modest home can be made to look permanent with careful site planning and landscaping. The single-wide is by far the most affordable form of home ownership—the most square feet for your buck, so to speak.

try. We see our job as "customer education," and as such, we're not about to mince words when necessary.

At the same time, we are addressing those in the industry with information about the consumer's needs—not to show how they can squeeze more profit out of them, but how they can help them get into a home that meets their needs. Our hope is that all those in the industry who read these pages walk away with a bit more understanding of what it is like to go through the buying process and make it a satisfactory "deal" on both sides of the equation.

The section of the book devoted to negotiation and how to establish the least amount of profit a dealer is willing to take is not there because we feel the dealer doesn't deserve to make a living, but simply to level the playing field: *you* deserve to get a fair deal too!

Our biggest concerns lie with the dealerships, and the businesses that own several dealerships, with in-house financing and insurance divisions. Each of these areas should be profitable, but just the same, each of them should be competitive: the home should not cost more than one from the competition, but neither should financing, nor insurance, nor the land and contractor services.

It gets nasty and unfair to the buyer when any of the following tactics are used:

Fig. 1.4. Still by no means the high end of modern manufactured housing, but certainly more residential looking: A double-wide with attached garage sitting on a poured concrete foundation, and again set in a nicely landscaped site.

❏ Dealers using covert sales tactics and withholding pertinent information from the buyer.

❏ Manufacturers and dealers fighting over who is responsible for different warranty areas of the home.

❏ Poorly trained sales people and dealers who don't give honest information, trying to gouge home buyers and not offering options—financing options, insurance options, contractor options, etc.

❏ Manufacturers and retailers still peddling "down and dirty trailers," that is, homes built to the absolute minimum of the HUD code.

❏ Insufficient regulation and enforcement of laws governing home set-up and the licensing of set-up crews.

We do not want to put down hard-working salespeople trying to make a living. We've been among their ranks ourselves. However, not all salespeople work hard and not all care about you, but most do want to see the people who do business with them happy. The nature of sales is stressful. Sell something or get fired. Too many salespeople operate in survival mode and see a potential sale as just that: a sale. They forget

Fig. 1.5. A triple-wide manufactured home with a spacious garage added to the far side of the home. The dormers over the living area and entryway give this home its site-built appearance.

that the sale has a name and a life attached to it. This survival mode can be a natural outcome of the sales profession and is exacerbated by the pressure from the dealership the salespeople work for.

Instead of general managers and sales managers demanding monthly and yearly quotas from each salesperson, they should train those sales people, and give them the proper tools that enable them to actually help every customer who walks through the door accomplish home ownership. That would mean helping the buyer obtain the best financing and payment terms, selecting the right options, and ensuring thorough follow-through once the customer has taken possession of the house. Doesn't that sound like a good company mission statement?

The majority of our time in the business was spent at one of the better dealerships, one that was sincere about customer satisfaction, but we have also been employed by a large corporation that didn't. We have also spent time at the factory level, so we do have the full picture to give you proper insight into the entire industry. We suggest you visit the factory that builds the brand of home you are interested in purchasing. Take this book with you and take thorough notes. Between this

Fig. 1.6. The hillside location of this double-wide suggested the use of a basement and an upper story deck, which turn this manufactured home into an impressive residence that compares well with any site-built construction costing 30–40% more.

book and that plant visit, you will learn much more than through talking to salespeople.

Our experience has been in the Pacific Northwest. You may have to adapt some of the information we provide to the part of the country where you live. For example, the "Super Good Cents" program for energy-efficient homes in the Northwest may have a different name where you live, or it may not exist at all.

The way you option your home and how it is set up will also vary. Many manufactured homes are set on solid, poured concrete foundations in the Northwest, much more often than, for instance, in the Southeast. Your insulation needs will vary, siding needs will vary, and even air conditioner needs will differ from region to region.

The one constant, however, is that dealers want maximum profit from you. A project this big won't always have an exact sequence, and glitches sometimes occur. Building permit hold-ups, undependable contractors, drawn-out financing, and a host of other variables can get in the way. However, this information will give you the knowledge needed to get the best home for your money, and work effectively with contractors.

If you have been through this process before, combine what you've learned from your own experience (and possibly your mistakes), with any new information you learn from this book, and your project will go much smoother, because you will be well prepared. Happy home hunting!

MHI photo

Fig. 1.7. Not your grandmother's "mobile home park" any more: This manufacturer's publicity photo shows how good a modern manufactured home development can look.

Today's Manufactured Homes

ANYONE CONSIDERING getting a new home built will be wise to at least consider the option of a manufactured home. What used to be called "mobile home," or even "trailer home," has reached a level of quality that does justice to its new name. By all means go by one or more dealerships and take a look at some of today's manufactured homes (don't leave your name and telephone number just yet, though). It will give you a first-hand impression of how these homes look and "feel" inside and out.

Manufactured Home Features

Manufacturers of these homes have realized that all types of potential home buyers would be interested in their homes—if they don't look like trailers with aluminum siding. Couple that with the indisputable fact that homes built on site are astronomically expensive and can take a year or more to build. Ever since the 1980s, as the cost of lumber has kept going up and up, more potential homeowners were stopped from achieving their goal of owning a "stick-built" house.

As for the quality of today's manufactured homes, manufacturers in different parts of the country started producing homes that met or surpassed the energy-efficiency standards of utility companies and new codes instituted for quality control.

The recent improvements in manufactured homes include 2 x 6 inch exterior walls, vinyl-clad dual-pane windows, insulation with high R-values, and hardboard siding. Even seasoned home buyers are taking note—imagine a house with all this "site-built" material for only $60 per square foot. But how much "site-built" quality is really built into one of these new manufactured homes—20%, 40%, or 80%? What are the components made of, and where do they come from?

Until 1976, the "trailer" industry built just that, trailers. Mobile homes varied in size from single-section homes measuring 8 x 40, 10 x 50, 10 x 55 and 12 x 60 feet to double-section homes that were 18 x 40 and 20 x 50 feet, among others. These homes had tail lights and hitches, used to move the homes to their site, but were never removed, and quite frequently became the base of a flower box.

Manufacturers did not have to comply with strict building codes or minimum standards. These mobile homes were typically built on two I-beams. The floor was built on top of them, and then walls and roofing were added. That may sound pretty much OK at first, because it's still done very similarly today. However, what was the floor made of? And how solidly built was it all? The exterior walls were often built with 1 x 2s, with the same aluminum siding used in RV construction. The roof was metal, with seams that needed sealing every fall, and the ceiling always leaked and was stained where the swamp cooler sat.

Windows were typically the famous three-tier roll-out louvered jobs that seemed to be open even when they were closed. The interior walls were perhaps one inch thick and had no sound insulation (nor was there much insulation in exterior walls, the floor, or the roof cavity).

The ceiling was barely seven feet from the floor, and the appliances, sinks, and fixtures were undersized, like something from the land of Lilliput.

The house was set on cinder blocks, and the gap was hidden with corrugated metal skirting.

The oil furnace always gave off fumes and never could keep up with the cold breeze that rushed through the house.

As you can tell, we turned this description personal, because one of us grew up in a 1965-model single-wide. It was like living in an oversized hallway. Thank goodness manufactured homes have improved a lot since those days.

However, there are still many things consumers should be aware of—quality of construction, financing, real estate concerns, installation matters, and, of course, price.

Everything presented to you here is a matter of fact. Manufactured homes are a great way to go in meeting your housing needs, but the industry is still growing and maturing. While it's good to know that retailers and manufacturers alike are prospering, that should not be at your expense.

Types of Factory-Built Homes

Sizes of manufactured homes vary from under 1,000 square feet clear up to 2,500 plus. There should be enough choices to fit everyone's needs. In this chapter, you will find some examples of popular floor plans. It is possible to modify floor plans to suit, but the factory will charge the dealer. The dealer will in turn charge you, the buyer.

As you will see, quality and the livability of manufactured housing have come a long way. The bigger double- and triple-section home plans rival those of any "site-built" home, and there are even 2-story homes available.

But first, let's see what defines a "manufactured home." Several different types of structures are built in the factory and designed for

Fig. 2.1. A larger manufactured home with an attached garage. (But see our comments in Chapter 5 for ways to make this kind of home even more attractive.)

19

long-term residential use. Here are the definitions adopted by the Manufactured Housing Institute:

Manufactured Home A home built entirely in the factory under a federal building code administered by the Department of Housing and Urban Development (HUD). The Federal Manufactured Home Construction and Safety Standards (the HUD Code) went into effect June 15, 1976. Manufactured homes may be single- or multi-section and are transported to the site and installed. These federal standards regulate manufactured housing design and construction, strength and durability, transportability, fire resistance, energy efficiency, and quality. The HUD Code also sets performance standards for heating, plumbing, air conditioning, and thermal and electrical systems. It is the only national building code.

Mobile Home This is the term that was used for manufactured homes built prior to June 15, 1976 (i.e., before the HUD Code went into effect). In many cases, particularly in North Carolina, these homes were built to voluntary industry standards.

Modular Home A factory-built home that is built to the state, local, or regional code where the home will be located. Multi-section units are transported to the site and installed.

Left and facing page: Figs. 2.2 & 2.3. Manufactured homes are built on a steel chassis made up of I-beams for each section. Fig. 2.3 shows the chassis with the floor joists installed.

Palm Harbor Homes photo

Panelized Home	A factory-built home in which panels—e.g. a whole wall with windows, doors, wiring, and siding—are transported to the site and assembled there. The homes must meet state or local building codes where they are sited.
Pre-Cut Home	A factory-built home in which building materials are factory-cut to design specifications, transported to the site, and assembled there. Pre-cut homes include kit, log, and dome houses. These homes must meet local or state building codes.

In this book, we are only dealing with the first category listed, the manufactured homes built entirely in a factory to the standards defined in the HUD Code, and transported in one or more complete sections to the homeowner's site.

About HUD and Building Codes

In 1974, the U.S. Department of Housing and Urban Development (HUD) was designated as the agency to oversee the Federal Manufactured Housing Program. The entity within HUD that is responsible for the oversight function is the Office of Consumer and Regulatory Affairs, Manufactured Housing and Standards Division.

A manufactured home (formerly "mobile home") is built to the Manufactured Home Construction and Safety Standards (the "HUD

Code") and displays a red certification label to that effect on the exterior of each section.

Most states have a State Administrative Agency (SAA) that administers the HUD Program in that state, and their addresses can be found on the Internet.

Left: Fig. 2.4. A look at longitudinal floor joists at the beginning of the factory line, shown here after under-floor insulation is installed.

Below: Fig. 2.5. This is the next stage, when the floor decking is installed on the floor joists.

Facing page: Fig. 2.6. Plumbing is installed before the floors, and later the walls, are insulated.

The Uniform Building Code (UBC) is a set of requirements that apply to the construction of site-built homes and is adopted by most states and counties. The UBC is stricter than the HUD Code regarding certain aspects of building.

Basic Frame Construction

The one thing that has been a constant in the construction of manufactured homes is the steel I-beam chassis on which the home is built. Whether it is a single-section, double-section, or triple-section home, each section has two I-beams running the full length. The size of these I-beams can vary from 8 to 12 inches, depending on the length and weight of the home. These steel beams, called the "chassis system," serve two purposes. One is to form the support for the "floor system." The wood floor system is attached to the I-beams. They give the home torsional stiffness (resistance against twisting), while allowing appropriate "give" during transport from the factory to the home's destination.

The second reason the steel I-beam chassis is used is quite simple: there has to be a place to attach the axles and wheels to move the home from the factory to your site. You might say the steel I-beam chassis is

integrated into the entire floor system. We have encountered people who wanted to set their manufactured home on a basement and then remove the I-beams. Not only is this against federal law, but as any structural engineer can tell you, there would be no practical or safe way to set the home on the basement without the I-beam structure. Plus, you can kiss your warranty good-bye.

The Way They Are Built

Typically, manufactured home factories are mere assembly lines with groups of workers doing the same function day in and day out. The home or section is pulled down the "line" and stopped for a specified amount of time. The line is moved again at the sound of a long whistle and flashing lights. Each stage of building is to be complete at each stop (this doesn't always happen, but for the most part, factories are fairly efficient and not much overlap occurs).

Above: Fig. 2.7. A wall section is craned over to the assembly line.

Facing page: Fig. 2.8. A view of the roof trusses before the roof decking is installed on them.

1. Once the floor system has been completed, the next step involves completing the plumbing and heating systems. The assembly line rolls on to the next stage, where the sheet vinyl ("linoleum") is laid across the whole width of the section and tacked down in the bathroom and kitchen areas. Then it's time to set the walls on the floor system. The walls are constructed in a different part of the plant and craned over to the "line." All four exterior walls are screwed into the floor and then the interior walls are added.

2. All the cabinetry is installed, along with sinks and fixtures. Different factories will add these smaller items at different stages.

3. The ceiling will be next, and like the walls, it is built at a different location in the plant and craned over to the line, where it is lowered and secured to the tops of the walls. In many cases, the drywall (also known by its common trade name Sheetrock) has already been textured before reaching this stage.

4. At this stage, for double- and triple-section homes, some manufacturers will temporarily join the sections together to make sure the interior walls line up, as well as to align any "crossover connections" that need to be made for electrical or plumbing connections. Not all factories do this step, but it avoids many potential problems later.

5. Now that the sections have been joined and the roof installed, much more begins to happen. The roofers hop to and begin laying shingles. Drywallers begin to hang drywall in the home. Tile counter edges are installed and other detail work is done.

6. Next, the crew arrives to put protective plastic over sensitive areas (sinks, fixtures, cabinets, electric panel boxes, etc.) to protect them from the rather messy process of spraying on the texture. This is the "mud" that goes on the walls and ceilings of homes on top of the drywall. The paint is usually mixed with the "mud" and applied at the same time.

7. Because the ceilings are usually textured separately from the walls, you will rarely get matching texture application from wall to ceiling. Some manufacturers are beginning to apply texture to walls and ceiling at the same time, but you will have to check.

8. Next, windows are installed and other detail work on the exterior is carried out. Sections that had been temporarily joined up under point 4 are separated, and the texture applicators step in to do their work. During completion of the texture, the exterior of the house gets painted if the home has hardboard siding.

9. Next is the application of paint. Unfortunately, most manufactured homes are not painted as well as they should be. Many manufacturers apply only a single thin spray coat of paint, whereas they

Fig. 2.9. The framing for a dormer with clerestory windows for a more elaborate home.

should really use a primer first. If the home is to have vinyl or cement lap siding, it is applied at this stage. If done correctly, the manufacturer first applies some type of backer before the siding is installed.

10. Shutters, window trim, any decorative trim or columns for the exterior front of the home, and light fixtures come next in the process.

Left: Fig. 2.10. Inside view of an exterior wall. Here you see an electrical outlet box nailed to a stud, which is better than the so-called "remodel box," which gets attached to the drywall only.

Below: Fig. 2.11. Roofing shingles are applied to the roof decking.

11. The home is near completion, and quality control should be going through each section, looking for defects before the home leaves the factory. Many times, however, defects get fixed in the field, i.e., at your site.

12. Once the home is completed, it is pulled from the factory to a staging area where it should be system-checked. Systems such as electrical and plumbing are checked. Natural gas systems are checked for leaks.

13. After completion of all tests, a red HUD tag is attached to the back of each section, showing that it has passed inspection, and the home is taken to the site.

14. If it is a multi-section home, it is pushed and pulled together at the "mating-" or "marriage-line." Ten- or twelve-inch-long lag bolts are used to join the roof ridge and the floor, while smaller lag bolts are used in the walls. The set-up crew should have put insulation between the sections all around the marriage line.

15. Next, the dealer begins sending in the various subcontractors to do the necessary finish work prior to the buyer's "move-in."

This is a general sequence, subject to change due to individual order variations. With all the factories around the country, there will be some

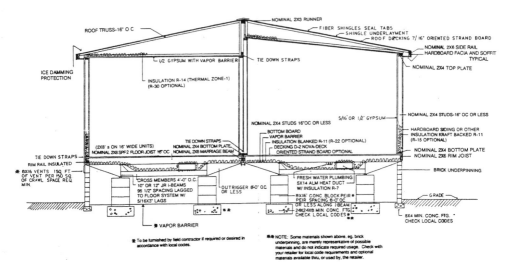

Fig. 2.12. Detailed cross section of double-wide on perimeter foundation.

deviations. For instance, some builders put the axles and tires on the chassis after the house is completed, while others put them on the chassis first. Some factories have a chain-driven assembly line that moves the homes smoothly and keeps them level, whereas others may hook the home to a forklift to move it to the next stage. In some factories, many stages of the building process go on outside, exposed to the weather, and some manufacturers even store their building materials outside, because their factory building is too small for storage.

Single, Double, Triple, and More...

Whereas originally most, if not all, manufactured homes were built in a single section, today the majority of homes are built as multiple-section homes. The latter look a lot more residential and offer more floor plan options, which will be covered in some detail in Chapter 3.

The standard single-section home ("single-wide") is a little less than 14 ft. wide and can be anything up to 80 ft. long.

When two sections are connected side-by-side, it's a two-section home ("double-wide"), which will be about 27 ft. wide and typically 40–60 ft. long, giving the home a more residential appearance, as well as more floor-plan flexibility.

Three sections joined side-by-side result in a three-section home, or "triple-wide," which is often indistinguishable from a site-built ranch-style home. Whereas on a double-wide the two sections are usually the

Fig. 2.13. Double-wide manufactured home before the siding is installed on the end wall. The end walls of this home are being finished at the site, instead of at the factory, providing a more "seamless" appearance.

same length, triple-wides usually have one section that is shorter or longer than the others, giving the home a less "boxy" appearance.

Whatever the number of sections, they can be enhanced with "pods," smaller sections attached to the side of the main section(s). These too help give the house more character as well as offering a more flexible layout. There are also dormers, which don't add space, but enhance the home's appearance

Of course, everything has its price. A simple single-wide offers the most "bang for the buck" (or rather, you pay "fewer bucks per bang"). This is where those mystical figures of $60 per square foot are to be found.

Adding more sections and/or pods increases not only the overall price, but also the price per square foot. Just the same, they all offer good value for the money, costing a lot less than similarly sized conventional homes.

Recently, more and more manufacturers have started offering two-story manufactured homes. This gives the home an even more residential appearance and more "livability," at least for those fit enough to climb stairs. Usually these two-story homes are created by finishing the main sections with stronger exterior walls and without a roof, and hoisting another section, with a peaked roof, on top of it. That calls for a bit more structural rigidity for the main sections, as well as interior and exterior staircases, and a more complicated roof line—read: more dollars per square foot for the added space, or "more bang, more bucks."

Fig. 2.14. Lego-block representation of the basic manufactured home configurations: single-wide with and without pods, double-wide, triple-wide, and two-story homes.

From an energy-efficiency standpoint, the more closely the home approaches the proportions of a cube (length, width, and height all about the same), the more energy-efficient it will be overall, given the same insulation levels (referred to as "R-values") for walls, floor, and roof.

Consequently, the single-wide should probably be avoided in regions with very high summer and/or low winter temperatures. At least theoretically, the two-story double-wide configuration should afford the highest relative energy efficiency.

On the other hand, energy efficiency is relative to the home's interior volume, so a small home can still be heated or cooled more cheaply than a larger one. As energy costs continue to soar, the advantages of living in a modest-size home should become more and more obvious.

Selecting a Floor Plan

I N THIS CHAPTER, we'll take a closer look at some of the typical configurations presented in Chapter 2, and discuss their respective advantages and disadvantages, if any.

The standard width of each section is usually quoted as 14 ft. In
fact it's usually no more than 13 ft. 8 in., due to limitations of permissible vehicle widths on the roads. Larger sections do exist, but they require special (and therefore more expensive) handling. Since the walls
are about 7 inches thick all around, that leaves the inside section width
at about 12 ft. 6 in.

The main aspect to keep in mind when selecting a floor plan is
what is referred to as "circulation": how to get in and out of the house
as well as from one room to another in the most logical way without
unnecessary traffic. To give an example, if you consider the living
room the center of the house, think which rooms you want to reach
most easily (i.e. most frequently) from there—probably the kitchen/
dining area and at least one bathroom. Those rooms should be connected as directly as possible. The bedrooms, on the other hand, aren't
visited so frequently, so it's OK if they are less directly connected.

Another example is the connection between the kitchen and the
outside world on the one hand and any utility area (e.g. laundry room)
on the other. You'll want access to the kitchen without traipsing the
groceries through the living room, and you'll want easy access to the
dining room and utility room from there. Try to think through the

functionality of any "standard" floor plan, both for comparison with other homes and to determine which changes you want to request at the time you order the home.

Since usually only the exterior walls are load-bearing walls, there is almost unlimited possibility of interior rearrangements—as long as you specify them before the manufacturer starts work on your home. Specify your changes when ordering, and don't accept unreasonable additional costs, because it generally doesn't cost the manufacturer any more. They may try to charge you an "engineering fee," but since you're not the first and only customer to request any particular change, all that presumed engineering work has already been done and paid for.

One change that should always be available at no additional cost is "flipping," or "mirroring"the floor plan, i.e. putting what's on the left on the right and vise versa.

Room-Specific Requirements

Whatever the number of sections of the home, and whatever the number of rooms it has, a few things should be met in any floor plan, and we suggest you insist on the following.

1. First, there's a bare minimum room size: that's 9 ft. in width, and of course the length must be more than the width. Anything less than 9 ft. wide isn't a room but a closet. And, talking about closets, the built-in closet that's needed for a room te be a bedroom must not protrude into the room.

   The only way you can get away with a room that's about 9 ft. square is if there is at least a 2 ft. 6 in. square entry nook into which the door opens. Since most manufacturers tend to overstate room sizes, they may try to include this area to the length of the room as though it were full-width, which of course it isn't. You can see an example of this practice in the bottom single-wide floor plan in Fig. 3.3, on page 37, for what is billed there as "Bedroom No. 3" of that otherwise very spacious single-wide. That glorified broom closet is quoted as 8 ft. 6 x 11 ft. 3. So allowing 3 ft. for the closet, and the door to open, leaves this room at 8 ft. 6 x 8 ft. 3—inadequate in all respects.

2. The next issue is closet size. Unless the closet door is as wide as the entire closet, the closet must be at least 2 ft. 6 in. deep, but preferably 3 ft. or more. If the closet is 2 ft. deep, and e.g. 4 ft wide with a 30-in entry door, it will be impossible to reach the items on either side of that door opening. Ideal is of course a true walk-in closet. In an L-shape configuration, a walk-in closet must be at least 5 ft. square, while a U-shape walk-in closet should be at least 6 ft. square, but preferably 6 ft. x 8 ft.

3. Now for the kitchen. The most efficient arrangement for a small kitchen is an L-shape configuration, which requires a minimum size of 9 ft. x 9 ft. At least one of the two sides without counters, cabinets, and appliances should be open to the dining area and to the utility room or the rear entry to the home. Larger kitchens, at least 9 ft. x 12 ft., can have a U-configuration. But again, there should be generous (at least 3-ft. wide) access to both the dining room and the utility area.

4. As for the bathrooms, the minimum size for a bathroom is 5 ft. x 7 ft. 6 in. Unfortunately, many home buyers are concerned only about getting a large (read: larger than necessary) master bath, and only too often that's compensated by a pathetically undersized second bathroom. A standard tub is 5 ft. long by 2 ft. 6 in. wide, and it takes a 5 ft. by 7 ft. 6in. room to squeeze it in with a toilet, a vanity, and a door opening. Smaller tubs and bathrooms may be OK for an RV, but not for a home, regardless whether it's conventionally built or a manufactured home.

   We've seen floor plans with two tiny bathrooms. It's much more practical for shared use to have what's referred to as the "split bathroom" configuration: equip one of those tiny rooms with only a tub and a sizable vanity (no toilet), the other one with a toilet and a vanity (no tub). The minimum size for those two rooms would be 5 ft. x 5 ft. and 3 ft. 6 in. x 5 ft. respectively.

5 Any home should have a utility room, even if it's only a ventilated closet space for the washer and dryer. Larger utility rooms should also house the water heater, the heating furnace, a utility sink, and cleaning materials closet. The logical place for the utility room is near the back of the house, directly accessible from the kitchen. If

space is at a premium, as it will be in any single-wide, consider getting a stacked washer and dryer and a tankless, or "flow-through" hot water system.

Single-Wide Floor Plans

Single-section homes, or "single-wides," are the simplest type of manufactured homes. They are also the cheapest, all else being equal. Their cost per square foot is lower, their transportation cost is lower, and their set-up cost is lower than is the case for the other types. On the down-side, they also look more like trailers—of course. Just the same, with careful attention to details, they can look as good as any other home.

In fact, whereas a small single-wide may look OK, because the balance between width and length is not too extreme, the larger ones start to look unbalanced. Although they're OK for a one- or two-bedroom unit, anything larger is also less practical inside, because you have to go through, or squeeze by, one room to get to another. For a vacation home that may be acceptable, but it's not much fun in a permanent residence.

The economy of single-wides is mainly due to the fact that the entire unit gets built and finished in the factory, whereas all multiple-section homes have to be assembled and finished on the site. Structurally their simple construction also makes it possible to make the unit strong and rigid enough without having to resort to larger-section lumber and other reinforcing and rigidifying means. And of course, it is cheaper to transport and install one section than it is for two or three.

In a single-wide, all you usually have to work with is that standard section width of 13 ft. 8 in. So your maximum inside width will be 12 ft. 6 in. That will also be the maximum width of any room in that single-wide. Not big for a living room by today's standards, but adequate for everyday living for a single person or a couple.

Figs. 3.1 through 3.3 on page 37 provide some examples of single-wide floor plans. You will notice that the one at the bottom shows a width of 15 ft. 6 in. That makes it an "oversize load," resulting in some complications in transporting it. However, considering how big the resulting home is, this is certainly a very cost-effective way to get into a 1,200 sq. ft. home.

Of the three examples shown here, the one at the top is the most traditional, with the kitchen at one end and the (master) bedroom at the other. This is the same configuration as that of the early "trailer homes"—but with much more generous dimensions and of higher quality. We would not put too much faith in that second bedroom as anything except a den, an office, or a hobby room. The way it juts out into the living room means that every sound from the living room can be heard in there. What's nice about this simple configuration is its relatively balanced dimensions, its length being less than four times the width, giving it a reasonably residential look.

Once you go for a second bedroom, the most common solution is to put one at either end: Parents at one end and the kids (or the live-in in-law, for whom this arrangement is known in the trade as "mother-in-law layout") at the other. Of course this kind of layout cries out for a second bathroom, one near each bedroom. So obviously you're leaving "super-cheap" behind, and your single-wide gets to be pretty long. Compared to any other two-bedroom home, it's still a bargain, though.

One feature we don't particularly like about any of these floor plans (in fact about far too many floor plans out there) is the entrance straight into the living room. It's no fun to expose your living room directly to the outside cold or heat, rain or sleet, whenever someone enters or leaves. Not very energy-efficient either.

This configuration really needs an enclosed front porch, which would be an expensive site-built addition. To get around that problem, look into specifying the front door relocated, for example to a hallway leading into the living room. Specification changes like that are often easy and cheap enough to make at the time the home is ordered—unlike having that kind of change made once the home is installed at your site.

If the single-wide is enhanced with a pod (a small section attached somewhere along one side), be prepared to pay more, so it behooves you to consider carefully how best to use it. Before specifying it, ask yourself the question, "is this really worth the extra X dollars?"

If the answer is yes, our preference would be to use it as a fully enclosed entrance lobby with a half bath and wardrobe storage. This helps shield the rest of the home from the elements when the front door is opened, and it gives guests the use of a washroom without having to go through somebody else's bedroom first. However, you may decide to use it to obtain a breakfast nook, a larger living or dining area, a utility room, or what have you. Consider its chosen use to determine the most appropriate location for that pod.

Another important consideration in specifying the details of a single-section home is the location of windows and doors. Most of the windows should probably be where the better view is—front, rear, left, or right. However, another factor is that bedroom windows should not be in the middle of the outside wall, where the bed will go, but off to the side. Also consider the direction of sunlight. In hot parts of the country, it's not a good idea to orient the main windows facing south or west. Although it's usually quite nice to have the sun shining into

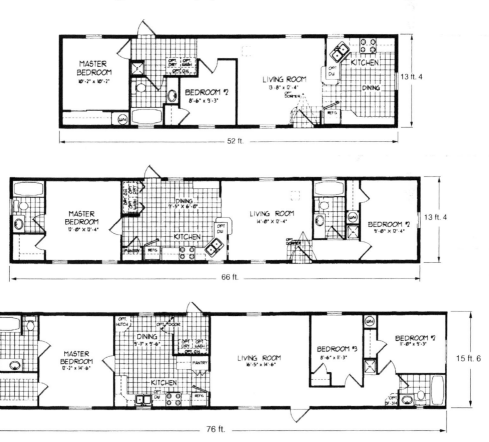

Figs. 3.1, 3.2, and 3.3. Three single-wide options. The one at the bottom is 15½ ft. wide, making it an oversize load, but offering a more liveable arrangement that's still cheaper than a double-wide of the same square footage.

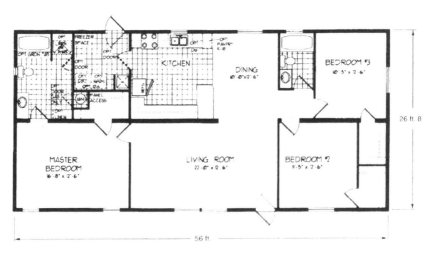

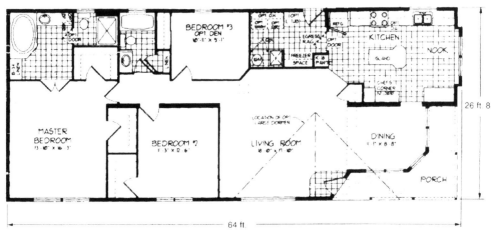

Facing page: Fig. 3.4–3.6. Examples of typical double-wide floor plans.

Top: Fig. 3.4. A modest 1,200 sq. ft. home with two bedrooms and two bathrooms. We don't like the way the dining area is tucked in between the kitchen and the laundry room. Instead, you should be able to specify the same home with the living room on the left, and the den between it and the kitchen, used as the dining room.

Middle: Fig. 3.5. A 1,500 sq. ft. three bedroom home with two bathrooms. This is a very efficient configuration with almost everything in the right place. and appropriately dimensioned. What more do you really need?

Bottom: Fig. 3.6. 1,700 square foot of manufactured-home opulence, but not so well designed. The second and third bedroom are too close to the living room, keeping the kids awake at night. The wrap-around deck is impractically narrow (the same square footage would be much more usable if it were a simple rectangular shape). And in a time of soaring energy and water costs, do you really need that swimming-pool size whirlpool bath in that oversize master bath?

Below: Fig. 3.7. Floor plan of a spacious quadruple-wide with three bedrooms.

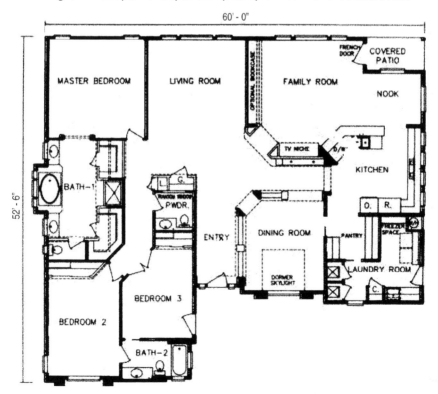

your home early in the morning, it's not so good during the hottest part of the day. By the same token, the entry doors should not face the direction of the prevailing wind, especially when it's raining, snowing, or freezing out there.

Double-Wide Floor Plans

Ever since the early 1990s, the majority of manufactured homes have been double-wides. At about 27 ft. wide, a double-wide is no smaller than many modest site-built homes, although to keep up with the current trend in "supersizing" homes, it takes at least a triple-wide to keep up with the site-built competition these days.

We're not believers in the "bigger is better" philosophy. We both grew up in very different homes, but both our families made do with only one living room and one dining room. We did just fine without a great room, a family room, a den, and a breakfast room. At today's soaring energy costs, it's time to reconsider the economy of such modesty. Cheaper to build, cheaper to furnish, cheaper to maintain—and more convenient to boot.

There are three good basic floor-plan configurations for double-wide homes:

1. Kitchen, utility room, and all bathrooms in one section, with living room and bedrooms in the other;

2. All bedrooms and bathrooms at one end, and the common areas at the other;

3. Master bed and bath at one end and the other bedroom(s) and bathroom(s) at the other.

Any of these arrangements will work just fine, depending on your personal preference. The most cost-effective, both in construction and maintenance, is the first one listed.

When different types of rooms seem to be placed randomly around the home, there is quite a lot of wasted space and unnecessary traffic through the house. Hot and cold water and drain lines run all around underneath the home, causing wasted energy and more plumbing noise everywhere in the house.

From a curb-appeal standpoint, double-wides tend to look better if the front section is shorter than the other, creating a stepped effect. The difference in length can be made up with an open front porch or a deck, as in Fig. 3.6. This gives the home a more residential appearance.

Triple-Wide and Bigger Floor Plans

Now you're really talking "outside the box." In most, though not all, cases, triple-wides and "quads"are much less boxy than the traditional manufactured home. This is achieved by making at least one section shorter or longer than the others. This will also provide greater flexibility in which way windows in various parts of the home can be oriented.

Choosing a floor plan with a long middle section gives maximum flexibility, providing the most direct access to the various rooms. It also tends to result in the most attractive appearance, especially if a non-symmetrical layout is selected (i.e., if the two side sections are not exactly of the same length as the center section).

Another alternate is to create an "inside" deck or patio by placing the shorter section between the two longer sections. This creates a pri-

Fig. 3.8. The intelligent floor plan. This home, designed and marketed by California architect Rocio Romero, has all the wet areas (kitchen, bathrooms, and utilities) in one section of the home, with the bedrooms in the other. A photograph of the finished home is shown on page 75.

vate deck area, which is especially desirable if the home is placed in a rather densely populated area, as in many manufactured home communities.

For very large homes, say 2,500 sq. ft. and more, there are quadruple-section homes, referred to as "quads." They come in sizes all the way up to about 3,000 sq. ft. They're hard to distinguish from site-built homes of the same size—at a significant savings in completion time (60 to 75% less) and financial outlay (15 to 35% less).

Finally, many of the bigger manufacturers now also offer two-story homes, and an example of such a floor plan is shown in Fig. 3.9.

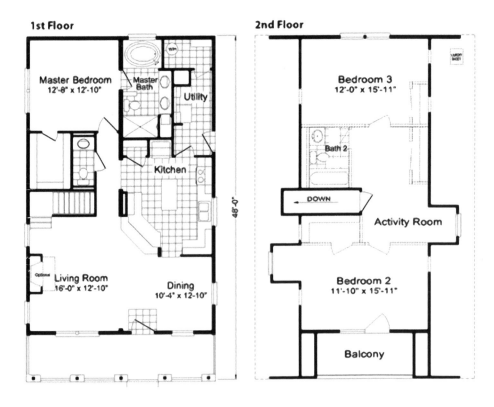

Fig. 3.9. Floor plan of a modest size two-story manufactured home. Basically it's a 1,140 sq. ft. double-wide with a 880 sq. ft. peaked-roof unit on top. It's delivered without walls in that top unit, allowing the owner to expand it (the floor plan shown here is only a suggestion).This arrangement offers considerably more flexibility, privacy, and pride of ownership than a double-wide of the same size. Depending on the exterior siding, it won't look out of place in any environment, from urban to rural. An exterior photo of this clever home can be found on page 165.

This type of home is often only available in certain regions. The floor plan shown as an example creates a nice cottage-style home, with the two children's bedrooms and second bathroom, as well as an open "activity area."

If you choose a two-story home, be very careful to check whether the stairs run in a logical, easily accessible location. We're not thrilled by the way they start next to the fireplace in the living room here. This turns your living room into a passage way. You don't want them to start right in your living room, dining room, or kitchen. They should start in a hallway from which you can access the common areas of the home.

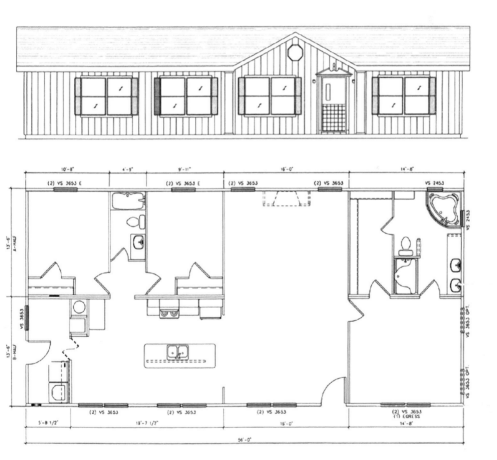

Fig. 3.10. Something new on the horizon? Floor plan and elevation sketch for a conceptual steel-framed 3 bed, 2 bath double-wide manufactured home, prepared by RADCO, Inc. for the Manufactured Housing Research Alliance in 2001.

4
Home Hunting

THESE DAYS, it is not uncommon to visit a manufactured home dealership and see a $160,000 triple-wide home. What happened to those $60 per square foot? Where has the idea gone of offering everyone the chance to become a homeowner of a quality home? What, if anything, have many manufacturers and dealers done to combat the

Fig. 4.1. An 1,800-sq. ft. double-wide, installed on a poured concrete foundation, ready for move-in. The dormer over the living area gives this home a "face." Though it still looks rather dull, some imaginative landscaping, especially at the left, will spruce it up very nicely.

high cost of lumber, materials, and labor? Actually, manufactured housing still gives you the opportunity to own more home for less money. However, as the quality has improved over the years, so has the cost.

Following the advice in this book, you can still get a good deal. but, as much as we'd like to reassure you, we suggest that before buying anything, you read each of the following chapters carefully, because unfortunately many manufacturers and dealers still leave some things out to bring you in.

As with many quickly changing industries, the manufactured housing industry has experienced growing pains—and, over the last several decades, "shrinking pains. These come in a variety of forms, including sales centers that are unprofessional and use high-pressure sales tactics. There is a high turnover of sales personnel and not enough after-sales follow-through. Manufacturers pressure the dealers to buy a certain number of homes. If the dealership can't meet the expected quota, they may finish up losing the brand and the holdback money (see the glossary on pages 180–181 for explanations of this and other unfamiliar terms).

Nevertheless, salespeople and owners of dealerships should understand that buying a home is the single largest purchase a family will make, and that the used-car-sales approach should be thrown out. Again, because of the enormous explosion in popularity of manufactured homes during the 80s and 90s, competition has become fierce and territorial. Thus, as a potential buyer, you need to be on your guard: Your pocketbook is their target.

Whether you are a first-time home buyer, an empty-nester, or a retiree, a manufactured home will work for you, but first you need to know these critical items:

1. Which dealer is reputable?

2. What brand and model is best for your needs?

3. How is the home constructed?

4. What type, brand, and quality of components are in the home?

5. What are the financing options?

6. Who will do the improvements on the property?

7. Who has the best price?

8. What options and upgrades should you order with the house?

9. What do you need to know about the contract?

10. How can you be in control of the buying process?

11. Is a "factory direct" dealership going to sell you a home for less?

12. How do you ensure service after the sale?

Knowledge is power. As you read these pages, mentally prepare yourself to be in control. You are not buying a home to make friends with a salesperson. Think about that 30-year mortgage you are taking on. You have to ensure you get the best home and service for your hard-earned money.

Below is a list of things you need to consider about each manufactured home you look at. Demand answers—confirmed in writing by the sales person—for each of these items. Beware, it's easy for a salesperson to orally confirm your question, and then later claim you must have misunderstood him. That's why you should write the answers down and have them confirm them with their initials and date.

Roof
◆ How are the shingles rated? Avoid anything less than 30-year rated.
◆ Are the shingles held down with nails or staples? They should be nailed, and how many nails per shingle?
◆ Are the shingles laid correctly, with an offset pattern, or are they lined up? Is there roof felt underneath the shingles?
◆ How thick is the roof decking that the shingles are attached to? It should be $5/8$ in.

Trusses and eaves
◆ What size are the trusses, and how far apart are they?
◆ How wide are the eaves, front, back, and ends?
◆ Is there ventilation under the eaves to allow the attic cavity to breathe?
◆ What kind of insulation is in the attic cavity?
◆ What is the R-value?

Siding	◆ If hardboard siding is used, what brand and type is it, and what is the warranty? ◆ Is it installed over a wind barrier (house-wrap), like Tyvek, and attached to plywood backer? ◆ If vinyl siding is used, is it installed over rigid plywood or oriented-strand board backer (and again over a wind-and-moisture barrier)? ◆ What kind of paint has been applied, and how many layers? ◆ What is the warranty on the siding material? ◆ Are the eaves and fascia hardboard, even though the siding is vinyl? ◆ What type of shutters come with the vinyl siding?
Exterior Walls	◆ Are the exterior wall studs 2 x 6, 16 inches on center? ◆ What is the R-value of the insulation in the exterior walls? ◆ Is the lumber in the house kiln dried? ◆ Is the bottom plate, or sole plate, of the exterior walls 2 x 6, 2 x 4, or 1 x 4?
Floors	◆ What size are the floor joists—2 x 6 or 2 x 8, and how far apart are they? ◆ Which direction do they run, longitudinally or transverse? ◆ How thick is the floor decking, and what is it made of and how is it applied—staples, screws, or nails? Is glue used in conjunction with the fastening method? ◆ What is the R-value of the insulation in the floor?
Windows	◆ What is the brand of the windows? ◆ Single-hung or (preferably) double-hung? ◆ Are they vinyl-clad, dual-pane windows with low-E glass? No need to go for argon-gas-filled windows—the gas seeps out in a few years.

Deck and Entry	◆ If your house has a built-on wooden deck, is it weather-sealed? ◆ If your house has a recessed entry, how "deep" is it? It should be 3 ft. minimum. ◆ What's under that indoor-outdoor carpet—marine plywood or regular floor decking?
Hitch	◆ Is the hitch removable? Make sure it is, if you want your home to look like a home.
Interior	◆ How thick is the drywall on the ceiling and the walls? ◆ How is it applied—with drywall screws or is it "foamed" on? ◆ Is the texture orange-peel (more attractive) or knockdown? ◆ Does the ceiling texture match the wall texture? ◆ Where the ceiling meets the top of the wall, is the joint filled with caulking or is it taped and textured, which will look much more attractive, especially after a year or so? ◆ What kind of interior paint is used, flat or semi-gloss? Flat is fine for the walls and ceiling, but the trim should be semi-gloss, which is also the better choice for kitchen and bathroom walls.)
Windows	◆ Are the window sills taped and textured or particle board wrapped with white or wood-grain vinyl, or, much better, painted wood? ◆ Are the window blinds plastic or, preferably, metal? Do the valances have a backing?
Carpet	◆ Don't take any carpet. Have the dealer omit it, because it's all low-quality "trailer" carpet. Have the dealer give you the somewhat meager credit, find out how many square yards are in the house, and pick out good carpet at a carpet store and have it installed professionally. Just add the price of the carpet to the purchase contract for the house.

Air Circulation and Ventilation

♦ Is the internal air exchange system passive or mechanical? Passive systems are quieter and more energy-efficient than mechanical systems.

Doors

♦ Are the exterior doors steel and insulated?
♦ Are they at least 32 inches wide?
♦ What kind of hinges are on the interior doors, mortised or cabinet-style hinges?
♦ How wide are the interior doorways?
♦ Are the doorknobs metal, as they should be, or plastic?

Bathrooms and Kitchen

♦ Are the bathroom wash basins plastic (yak…), metal, or vitreous china?
♦ Are the faucets plastic (yak, again) or metal?
♦ Are the tubs metal or fiberglass—hopefully not plastic?
♦ Do the bathrooms come with a towel bars and toilet paper holder?
♦ Are there tile back-splashes above all sinks and wash basins?
♦ Are there metal shut-off valves under the sinks and behind the toilets?

Fig. 4.2. The two sections of a double-wide manufactured home staged to be rolled over and then placed on the poured perimeter foundation and joined up.

◆ Is there a medicine cabinet in each bathroom?

◆ Is there strip lighting over the bathroom sink, or preferably sconces on either side of the mirror?

◆ Is there at least one GFI (ground-fault interrupt) electric outlet in the kitchen and each bathroom?

◆ What kind of floor covering is used in the bathroom and kitchen? Best is non-shiny ceramic tile (so you're less likely to slip), but commercial grade sheet vinyl is fine too.

◆ Are cabinets and cabinet doors made of wood or particle board? Insist on solid wood.

◆ What kind of laminate is used on counter tops in the home, and where are the seams located? Seams near the sink should be avoided.

◆ How deep is the sink in the kitchen? It should be no less than 8 inches. Is it stainless steel or enameled?

◆ Does the range hood have a light and a fan? What brands of appliances come with the house?

◆ Are there at least 18-inch-deep shelves or cabinets for laundry storage in the utility room or the washer-dryer area?

◆ Is there an outlet for a freezer?

◆ What brand and quality of sheet vinyl is on the floor in the kitchen and the utility area? Insist on commercial grade sheet vinyl or ceramic tile

Skylights

◆ Skylights are nice for brightening up areas near the center of the home, but:

◆ Make sure they have low-E glass panes— certainly not plastic—and are openable for ventilation and to prevent heat buildup.

◆ Specify adjustable light-filtering cellular or Venitian blinds for the skylights.

5
Financing:
Shop For the Money First

R EAD THIS CHAPTER slowly and carefully. Let its message soak into your skin and course through your veins. Why? Because financing is the place where you can save most money. Every dealer is out to make as much profit from you as possible—not only by asking for the highest possible purchase price, but through financing as well. Manufactured home dealers get a "kickback" at the end of the year from "in house" lenders. This kickback, or rebate, is one to two percent of every "deal" the dealership gets financed.

But first, let us give you some insider information on cash buyers versus financing. To the dealer, it's all the same. It doesn't matter to him whether you give him the money or the bank does. So paying cash does not guarantee a big discount, even if the dealer says something to that effect.

How much you pay for the money the bank lends you can make a huge difference in the total sum you end up paying for your home over the years. To show you what's involved, we'll follow an imaginary couple around as they shop for a home.

Today's interest rates are at historical record lows, and as long as you "shop" for financing first, you can benefit from that. In the rest of the chapter, we'll show you how to get a better deal by securing financing first, *before* shopping for the house.

A Scenario For Paying Too Much

Let's watch our imaginary typical couple—whom we'll call Travis and Tara—as they obtain financing while shopping for their home. They are first-time home buyers with good credit. They want to buy land and a new home for their new addition—their first child. They are good, dependable renters, who always pay the rent on time and have lived in the community for many years. They have also managed to save enough for a hefty down payment.

One Sunday they stop at a dealership with a big, bright sign in front that reads: "One-stop shopping! We finance and insure right here!"

Travis and Tara are fond of convenience, so they stop for a look. The salesman tells Travis and Tara that the dealership obtains financing and can provide homeowners' insurance as required by all lenders. Sounds good, doesn't it? Convenience is a wonderful thing. Now let's see what the convenience of one-stop shopping is going to cost Travis and Tara.

A. Home:

Purchase price of home $60,500

Air conditioner. $3,200

Subtotal $63,700

Tax at 7% $4,460

House total $68,160

B. Site:

Price of land. $35,000

Foundation, well, power, septic. $18,000

Site total $53,000

Total package price. $121,160

The finance companies that the dealership uses work on a simple premise—low down payment, high interest rates. So their salesman assures them there's no need to make that big down payment for which they'd been saving up. Instead, he says, treat yourself to a new car or use your cash for some other purpose. He can get them into that home with *"only 5% down!"* If that isn't saving them some big bucks...

Total land-home package price $121,160

Less 5% down payment . . . . −$6,060

Amount to finance **$115,100**

Typical finance company interest rate 7.75%

If Travis and Tara finance those $115,100 at 7.75%, their monthly payment is $780, not including tax and insurance. A reasonable figure to add is $300 per month to cover these items.

Monthly total **$1,030**

The dealer gets a kickback of about $1,725 from the lender.

How to Get a Better Deal

If, instead, Travis and Tara had gone to a bank, a credit union, or a mortgage broker first, they may have found they qualified for an 4.5% interest rate with a 10% down payment. If we recalculate costs, we discover that would have been a significantly better deal.

Land-home package price $121,160

Less 10% down payment. . . . . −$12,116

Amount to finance **$109,044**

Note: at present (2021), mortgage rates are significantly lower than the ones used in many of these examples, making this a good time to finance a new home (or refinance your existing home).

Financing $109,044 at 4.75% for 30 years, they would have a monthly payment of $553. Of course, they would still have to budget the additional $300 per month to cover tax and insurance.

Monthly total **$853**

Assuming they take the full 30 years to pay off their mortgage, they will pay a total of $280,800 in interest and principal if they finance with the dealership. If instead they finance with the 30 year 4.75% mortgage from a bank or a credit union, their total will be only $199,080. That's a total savings of $81,720.

Surely it's worth spending a couple of hours of your time to go to a bank and save those $81,720. Isn't it worth that time to reduce your total monthly housing outlay from $1,287 to $1,030 for the same home?

Alternately, if they really can afford that monthly payment of $987, they could pay off that 30-year mortgage in 16 years, and they'd own the house free and clear 14 years earlier!

The next thing that went wrong for Travis and Tara, which will be described in more detail in Chapter 7, is that they fell for the car dealership trick: "What kind of monthly payment are you looking for?" Answering that makes the customer an easy prey for a salesman.

Why is the payment approach flawed? The negotiation is based on a figure that came out of nowhere and is not based on the price of the home. Salespeople love this. If you, the buyer, reveal how much you're prepared to spend per month, the salesperson will figure a way to make you spend that much—and not a penny less.

If you went to a bank or mortgage broker and got approved for a loan first, you would know the maximum price of a home you could afford to buy. You'd be talking price, not monthly payments, and you could negotiate on the basis of the home's asking price, instead of having the dealer play cat-and-mouse with you.

There is another reason dealers like to finance home buyers with their in-house lenders: the dealer gets "funded" by the lender before your house is delivered to your site. The dealer achieves total control, and you are left to his whim. A very good reason to obtain financing somewhere else than at a dealership.

A Road Map to Better Financing

Here's a road map for a better route to home financing. But first, you need to know how qualified you are to get a conventional mortgage, and the first step there is to know your credit score, specifically, for our use, the FICO credit score, which can range from 300 (awful) to 850 (excellent).

Do not yield to the temptation of setting a foot onto a single sales lot until you have acquired your own copy of your credit report from all three bureaus. You can begin the process of acquiring all three of these reports at the same time by dialing the following toll-free number: 1-888-567-8688, which will guide you through the process. You will be required to provide a photocopy of your driver's license and, most likely, a utility bill to prove you're whom you claim to be and live where you say you do. By law, a dealer cannot give you a copy of the report they obtained on you. We can't emphasize this enough: Get your own credit reports!

By getting pre-qualified, you will know what payment you can afford and how much total you can borrow. We recommend visiting at least three sources to gather information. These sources can give you an estimate, and then give you an exact figure of the annualized percentage rate (APR) which you qualify for, as well as how much money you can borrow. Don't be shy about asking questions. Lending money is

Fig. 5.1. Manufacturer's cut-away view of a model of a high-end triple-wide manufactured home, complete with furnishing suggestions. A home like this will approach $150,000, but at today's mortgage rates, that's almost "affordable."

what keeps lenders in business, and answering your questions is part of their job.

Terms of the Loan

Should you finance for 30 years or 15 years? The answer to this question depends on your comfort level and what you have qualified for. Typically, 15-year mortgages are offered at slightly better APR than a 30-year mortgage for the same amount. Here's an example:

15 year loan per $100,000 borrowed

Interest rate (APR) 7.50%
Monthly payment $927.01
Total payments $166,862

30 year loan per $100,000 borrowed

Interest rate (APR) 7.75%
Monthly payment $716.41
Total payments $257,908

Monthly difference $210.60
Total payment difference $91,046

If you are comfortable with spending $210.60 more a month to own your home in 15 years instead of in 30 years, then go for it: you'll save an incredible $91,046 in the long run. If not, you can always take a 30-year mortgage and make one or more extra payments a year. By making just one extra payment per year, you will pay off your 30-year mortgage in less than 23 years. But: whenever you send in that extra payment, you *must* specify it to be used "in payment of principal only."

Variable Interest Rates

Variable interest rates, which go up and down according to the prime lending rate, can be a real advantage—at times, but taken out at a time of low interest rates, they can be very scary. Be very careful: depending on the economy and the indicator your rate is tied to, your interest rate could go up (or down) quite drastically. It's OK at a time when interest rates are high (because they must be reduced immediately when their base indicator rate goes down, although they climb more gradually on the way up).

Graduated Interest Rates

Don't be tempted by the low initial payments offered with so-called graduated interest rates and rate sales. Graduated rates work like a step ladder. The rate starts low and then, year after year for the first three to five years, it increases incrementally.

Dealers like to offer programs like this to first-time buyers to "help them get into a home more quickly," alluding to the assumption that you'll be earning more money five years down the line, allowing you to meet those higher payments then.

How does a starting rate of 7% sound? Pretty good, you think? However, see what a rate that starts at 7% and goes to 11% over 5 years on a $100,000 loan does to your monthly payment schedule:

1st year: $665.30/month

2nd year $733.76/month

3rd year: $804.62/month

4th year: $877.57/month

5th year and all following years: $952.32/month

When you look at it this way, it doesn't look so good, does it? At the end of the day, that $100,000 loan will have cost you a whopping $334,100!

If you are a first-time home buyer and have found out you have good credit, you can qualify for a 3% or 5% down payment program through a reputable bank or mortgage broker and get the current "conforming" interest rate. To get more specific loan and interest information, a good web site to check is *http://www.bankrate.com*.

Let's explain the term "conforming," which you'll frequently hear as you are going through the financing process. Conforming loans are ones that meet all the lender's guidelines. An example would be a home buyer with "excellent type A" credit who meets all the other criteria set forth by the lender to obtain a mortgage to buy a home or home-land package.

There are many lenders who will lend money to people with less than perfect, non-conforming, credit—that is, B, C, or D credit. These loans require a higher down payment and will have higher interest rates. However, in many cases, after just 24 to 36 months of making your mortgage payments on time, and keeping up with any other payments, you may be able to re-finance at a low conforming interest rate.

Figuring What Your Payments Buy

Table 5.1 is a chart to determine what a certain payment will buy in a lump sum of money.

Here's how to use that table: Divide what you plan to pay per month by the payment per $1,000 borrowed from this table, then multiply by 10,000 (that is simply done by moving the decimal point 4 places to the right).

Here's an example. Say you've figured you can afford to spend $500 per month for 30 years, and the interest rate is 6.5%.

1. In the left-hand column find the length of the term; then move over to the column with the applicable interest rate, and read off $63.21.

2. $500 divided by $63.21 equals 7.91.

Table 5.1. Monthly payments in $ per $1,000 borrowed

Term of loan	6.0% APR	6.5% APR	7.0% APR	7.5% APR	8.0% APR	8.5% APR	9.0% APR	9.5% APR	10% APR
15 years	$84.38	$87.11	$89.88	$91.70	$95.56	$98.47	$101.42	$104.44	$107.46
20 years	$71.64	$74.56	$77.53	$80.56	$93.94	$86.78	$89.97	$93.24	$96.50
25 years	$64.43	$67.53	$70.68	$73.90	$77.18	$80.52	$83.92	$87.36	9$0.80
30 years	$59.95	$63.21	$66.53	$69.92	$73.38	$76.89	$80.46	$84.11	$87.76

3. Move the decimal point 4 places to the right: $500 per month at 6.5% will buy you $79,100.

Once you can use this chart, you will know more about financing than most salespeople.

Let's try another example: $600 monthly payment for 25 years at an 8% interest rate.

1. From the table, read off 77.18

2. $600 divided by 77.18 = ... $7.7740

3. Loan amount: move the decimal 4 places to the right = . . . $77,740

It's vital to know and understand that a monthly payment "buys" a lump sum of cash. After you are qualified at your local bank, and you know what you can spend—and more importantly, how much you are comfortable spending—per month, you won't have to rely on a salesperson to calculate any such figures for you.

Once you are comfortable calculating from this chart, sit down and think about how much house and money you need. We would suggest you take what you want to spend per month on your home, and add all other debt payments to it. Add only the minimum monthly payments to the house payment. Don't count utility bills, food, etc. Just credit cards, child support, car payments, etc. Here's an example:

House payment $750
Car payment and furniture $320
Credit card payments $100

Total **$1,170**

Divide $1,170 by your gross monthly income. Say your total household income is $3,500 per month. Take $1,170 and divide by 3,500; that equals 0.33, or 33%. If the answer exceeds 36%, you simply can't afford to buy that much house, unless you pay off some of those existing bills first. Ignore anything else a dealer may tell you. The dealer's interest is in making the highest possible profit, not what's best for you.

Dealing with Points

A word about points. We don't recommend them. What points do is buy a lower interest rate. Generally one point (1%) of the amount you are financing will lower your interest rate by one quarter of a percent. It can be confusing and causes the closing costs of your loan to be higher. Manufactured home dealers love points, because the finance companies they work with will actually add the cost of your points onto your loan amount. Isn't that a bit self-defeating? It doesn't make much sense to reduce your interest rate while at the same time increasing your loan amount, does it? Even points at a bank or credit union are something to avoid.

Mortgage Types Compared

The *Mortgage Money Guide*, published by the Federal Trade Commission, urges home buyers to use a comparison and quick-check chart to determine which type of mortgage will work best for them.

30-Year Fixed-Rate Mortgage

Fixed interest rate, long term:

Pros: Stable payments and long-term tax advantages.

Cons: Interest rate can be a bit higher than other kinds of financing.

15-Year Fixed-Rate Mortgage

Fixed interest rate, shorter term:

Pros: Equity in your property will be gained more quickly.

            Interest rates usually lower than with a 30-year mortgage.

Cons: Higher monthly payments than a 30-year mortgage.

May require a higher down payment than a 30-year mortgage.

Adjustable-Rate Mortgage ("ARM")

Interest rate changes over the life of the loan:

Pros: Beginning interest rate is below market.

                 Rate caps can limit payment increases.

Cons: Payments can increase suddenly.

Balloon Mortgage

Fixed-rate, short term; the payments may cover interest only, with the loan amount due in full at a specified time.

Pros: Can offer low monthly payments.

Cons: Chance of no equity until loan is paid in full.

Graduated Interest Rate Mortgage (or "Payment Mortgage")

Monthly payments rise gradually, then stabilize for the rest of the loan:

Pros: This loan can be easier to qualify for.

Cons: Your income must keep pace with the payment increase.

Shared Appreciation Mortgage

Below-market rate and low monthly payments in exchange for a share of profits when property is sold:

Pros: Low rate, low payments.

Cons: If the property appreciates, the cost of the loan goes up.

                 If the property depreciates, the projected increase in value may still be due.

Figuring Out What You Can Afford

Table 52, below, shows the maximum monthly amount you may have available for home payments and total monthly obligations depending on your annual income. No more than 28% of your gross monthly income (before taxes) should be used for mortgage payments (principal, interest, taxes, insurance, and mortgage insurance). No more than 36% of your gross monthly income should be going toward your mortgage payment plus all other monthly obligations (car loan, credit cards, etc.).

A more modern way of checking what you can afford is shown in Fig. 5.2 on page 63, using the app found on the Fannie Mae website, *http://www.fanniemae.com.*

Calculating Your Mortgage Payment

The following tables will tell you what the monthly payments will be for different interest rates and terms (principal and interest). For example, a monthly payment for a $60,000, 30-year fixed loan at 8% would

Table 5.2. Monthly payment based on income

Total annual income	Monthly mortgage payment	Monthly total credit obligations
$20,000	$467	$600
$30,000	$700	$900
$40,000	$933	$1,200
$50,000	$1,167	$1,500
$60,000	$1,400	$1,800
$70,000	$1,633	$2,100
$80,000	$1,867	$2,400
$90,000	$2,100	$2,700
$100,000	$2,333	$3,000

(Source: *Unraveling the Mortgage Loan Mystery*, Federal National Mortgage Association.)

be $440.26. For amounts over $100,000, add two payments together that equal the numbers for the amount borrowed.

Example:

$125,000 loan, 8% interest, 30 years:

First find the payment for $100,000,then the payment for $25,000, and add the two together for the total monthly payment of principal and interest.

$100,000 payment $733.76
$25,000 payment $183.44

$125,000 payment: $733.36 + $183.44 = ... **$917.20**

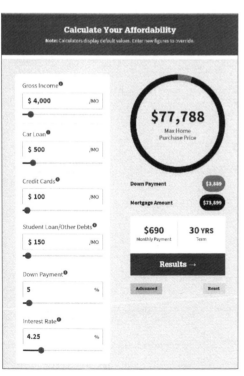

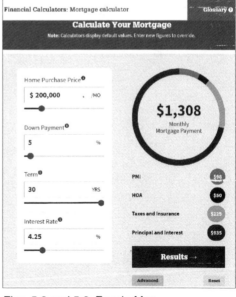

Figs. 5.2 and 5.3. Fannie Mae calculator apps for affordability and mortgage payments. Explanations at *http://www.fanniemae.com.*

Speeding up Your Loan Application Process

The Federal National Mortgage Association, otherwise known as Fannie Mae, says these are some things a lender will look for as documentation from you:

Source of down payment	It may come from savings, sale of property, or life insurance properties. It can also be from relatives if it doesn't have to be repaid, depending on the loan program.
Current debts	Names and addresses of current creditors, monthly payments and balances. Bank statements may be required.
Current assets	Account numbers and balances and names of financial institutions for checking, savings, and investment accounts. Real estate and personal property can be listed on your application.
Sources of income	Two recent pay stubs and your W-2 forms for the previous two years are good verification. You must verify income from social security, pensions, dividends or interest, and rental income.
Employment information	Name, address and phone number of all employers for the past seven years.
	Your addresses for the past seven years.

How Much Can You Borrow?

Table 5.3, on the next page, is a chart from Fannie Mae that shows how much income you need to get a mortgage. Before the 2008 mortgage cricis, many lenders used more lenient guidelines and may have required less income, but you would pay with higher interest rates. Today's figures are more restrictive, but the upside is that since the 2010 recovery, mortgage rates have been at a historic low. The table is based on a 30-year loan with 20% down payment. It assumes property taxes equal to 1.5 % of the purchase price and hazard insurance of 0.25 % of purchase price.

Today, there are easy caculator apps for computers or smart phones, and an example is shown in Figs. 5.2 and 5.3, which can be found at *http://www.fanniemae.com*. (Even so, we still like using tables, because they show not only the one figure you need, but also give you an idea of what a little more or a little less interest would do for your situation.)

Financing and Loan Structure

A land-home package can close a couple of different ways. It is important that you know which way your loan is structured.

1. The loan closes after the home is installed and all improvements are completed. Final appraisal is done, and the loan closes at the title company. Everyone is funded (land owner, dealer, contractors).

2. First there is a closing on the land to pay the seller; then, after improvements are done and the house is installed, there is a final inspection, followed by a second closing whereupon the remaining money is funded to the contractors and the dealer.

Table 5.3. Annual income requirements based on amount borrowed and interest rate

Interest Rate	Loan Amount				
	$50,000	$75,000	$100,000	$150,000	$200,000
6%	$16,754	$25,131	$33,508	$50,261	$67,016
6.5%	$17,451	$26,176	$34,901	$52,352	$69,802
7%	$18,163	$27,244	$36,325	$54,488	$72,750
7.5%	$18,889	$28,334	$37,779	$56,668	$75,558
8%	$19,630	$29,445	$39,260	$58,889	$78,520
8.5%	$20,383	$30,574	$40,766	$62,149	$81,532
9%	$21,148	$31,722	$42,296	$63,444	$84,592
9.5%	$21,925	$32,887	$43,849	$65,774	$87,698
10%	$22,711	$34,067	$45,423	$68,134	$90,846
10.5%	$23,508	$35,262	$47,016	$70,523	$94,032
11%	$24,313	$36,470	$48,626	$72,940	$97,252
11.5%	$25,127	$37,690	$50,254	$75,380	$100,508

3. The loan is set for four or five draws. The dealer and certain contractors are paid upon completion of their particular specialty.

Inform your contractors of the kind of loan structure you have.

Insurance

Obviously you need some kinds of insurance. But from whom and for how much? From the dealership? Of course not. Insurance is required by all lenders, and the friendly dealership would probably be more than happy to sell you everything you need and more. However, if you buy it from them, you'll probably pay much more than you should.

There are two types of insurance that usually apply to your home-buying: regular homeowner's insurance and sometimes PMI, or "Private Mortgage Insurance." In addition to these forms of insurance, you may want to take out other forms of insurance.

First and foremost, you *do* need homeowner's insurance: flood, fire, physical damage, etc. Second, think about looking into credit life insurance and credit disability insurance. You may need additional insurance to pay off your loan should you pass away or become injured. Your payments would be made on your behalf. Some dealerships conveniently add these premiums to your loan, which increases your loan amount, so you end up paying more per month.

Seek out an insurance agent for your homeowner's insurance and get two or three quotes. These will be your best bets. Your bank or credit union will have some of the best rates on credit, life, and disability insurance. Think hard about credit insurance. If you're in good health and under 50, you probably won't find it a good buy. Remember, you don't have to take the insurance from the bank you're getting your loan from. Feel free to shop around.

Homeowner's Insurance: How Much Do You Need?

You need to insure the cost to rebuild the home, then add on extras, such as the cost of central air conditioning, furnishings, appliances, etc. There are three types of homeowner's policies: "cash value," "guaranteed replacement cost," and "replacement cost."

Cash value is the cheapest. It pays you whatever your house and valuables would sell for today, which will probably not get you the same item years later. Guaranteed replacement cost insurance offers the best coverage, but it generally will not cover the cost of upgrading your house to meet building codes that have changed since the policy was initially put into force. Replacement cost insurance will replace items that were lost, but not always with the exact same item.

Homeowner's insurance also includes liability coverage up to $300,000. If your total assets (including your equity in the home) exceed $300,000, you should buy additional liability coverage to avoid losing your shirt (or, rather, your home) if you should ever get sued.

Private Mortgage Insurance

Private Mortgage Insurance is insurance that is required so that if you should die and there is nobody to pay back the loan, an insurance company pays the loan for you. If you put less than 20% down, the bank, credit union, or savings and loan will require you to pay thus monthly insurance premium. PMI can add as much as $65 to your monthly payment.

If you borrow $100,000 and make a $20,000 down payment, you can avoid PMI. However, many of us don't have that much to put down, so we end up paying more. Be sure to check on your equity from whomever services your loan, and cancel the PMI once it reaches 20%. The lender won't necessarily tell you and gladly keep collecting that PMI premium, required or not.

You may find, if you explore dealer financing, that their lenders don't normally require PMI. Why? Because the interest rate is so high that it causes monthly payments in turn to be so high that it can put the customer out of qualifying for the loan. Additionally, the high rate of interest makes a ton of money for the lender anyway, so it's worth the risk for them to waive the PMI.

Resale Value, Appreciation, and Depreciation

Many people are concerned with the appreciation of a manufactured home and its resale value. Here is what we have found to be the case:

When you purchase a manufactured home, it receives a title and registration because it is initially recognized as a vehicle by the state. If you place your manufactured home in a manufactured home community—or on private property for that matter—and it is installed above ground, resting either on blocks or jack stands, it will be regarded as personal property, much like a car. Generally, there will be no appreciation of value to the home.

However, when placed on a poured concrete foundation or basement on private land, you can convert it to real estate. It becomes what is called "appurtenant to the land"; in other words, the home becomes part of the real estate. When you go to the closing at the title company, you will sign a form called "Elimination of Title." This form does exactly what its name implies: it gets rid of the separate title to the home and converts it to real property.

Typically, your real estate then starts appreciating in value, as it has consistently done in the past. Unfortunately, that's not necessarily the case in times of recession, such as during the 2008-2010 housing crisis, when even real estate—especially real estate—was depreciating, or losing value, instead of increasing in value as it does during more prosperous times. However, it's worth hanging on to it if you can, because over the long run, your home will still maintain its value better than many other kinds of assets, *and* it provides you with a place to call home!

6
Finding a Good Dealer

IN MANY PARTS of the U.S., you can't swing a cat without hitting a manufactured home dealer. You may find 10 or 20 on the same road within 10 miles from each other. How do you find a reputable one? Take the word of a salesman on the lot? Hardly.

Before you buy, we suggest you do some homework first. Try to get to look at one or two manufactured homes that people are actually living in—relatives, friends, neighbors, friends of friends, anyone you feel comfortable asking. Get their feedback on their experience, both buying the home and living in it—as well as about the dealer and contractors they've done business with.

Time to Buy

When it gets to be time to seriously shop around for one yourself, first consider when to start the process.

Usually, salespeople and sales managers are pushing for monthly and yearly sales quotas. Sales people get "spiffed" if they reach a set goal of write-ups (i.e. sales) per month.

We suggest the end of any month or anytime in December to buy. A dealer may be less apt to pull the sales game with you, and just wants to close the deal, regardless of his commission on it.

One more good reason to buy at these times is that the owner of the dealership gets the coveted holdback check from the manufacturer at the end of the year. Many times this money is the better part of their yearly pay. It can range from hundreds to thousands of dollars per home. Here's an example:

Homes sold in one year: 100

Average invoice cost per home: $75,000

Holdback % per invoice: 9%

Total check due dealer from manufacturer:. $675,000

That's not a bad bonus for the year, is it? The bigger dealers, which can sell more of a particular brand, can negotiate the holdback with the manufacturer. It can be anywhere from 2 to 14% per invoice (i.e., per home sold).

Note:

Even the so-called "factory-direct" dealerships can have a hold-back calculated into the home's price.

Types of Manufactured Home Dealers

In the sections that follow, we'll take a look at the different types of manufactured home dealerships and compare what they can offer you.

"Environmental Display" Mega-Dealers

Just think of them as huge dealerships with huge overheads. Dealers don't normally own their display homes (or stock homes, ready for immediate delivery). They pay interest on them to flooring companies. This interest is high, normally prime plus 2 or 3 %. Auto dealers operate the same way. A reasonable figure for a dealer with 20 display homes and 10 stock homes would be $8,000 to $10,000 in interest per month. Then there's the power bill to pay, along with landscaping, commissions, and plenty of other overhead.

Think about walking into a home with no furniture. It's cold and the carpet isn't even down. Looks barren, doesn't it? It makes a fair impression at best, with not much value here to justify the price. However, if you walked into the same place set up as a display home, furnished, with all the lights on, a bit of potpourri in the air, and the table set, wouldn't you feel more value in that home?

Don't get caught up in it. Underneath, the furnished and set-up home is still the same home as the bare, unfurnished one, which is what you will be getting delivered to your site. Turn your buying process practical, not emotional.

More and more dealers are using this emotional technique, and it is working with the majority of customers. Buying is an emotional decision for most people, and dealers know it. They capitalize on it and will take all you have.

Don't fall for this environmental display ploy. This approach is the equivalent of test-driving a car. The whole concept is to get you in a furnished home and romance you into justifying the high price they are asking. They maximize the emotional context of the buying game. Unfortunately, lots of home buyers fall for it. Don't get charmed by the nice way the display home is furnished (called "staging") and the landscaping of the lot. Imagine that home empty, sitting on your freshly poured concrete pad instead. Think how you can (afford to) furnish and landscape it, not the way it is staged. Buyer beware.

"Mom and Pop" Dealerships

Now, let's turn to the small hole-in-the-wall dealer. Their lot is unkempt, the houses are pinch-parked, no carpet is laid, the doors haven't been squared and don't even shut. Here's a place to get a deal, you may think. The dealer's overhead costs may be less than they are for a larger dealer, but that does not necessarily translate into a better deal for the buyer. You still need to shop around and do your own legwork.

Let's give the dealer the benefit of the doubt. He may ask a thousand or so less than the competition, but he is still getting a rebate or kickback from the factory, just like the mega-dealer. He and the in-house finance companies may be making some extra bucks from contractor referrals. Still think you're going to get a good deal?

"Factory-Direct"

Finally, what's going on with this "factory direct" stuff? Over the last several decades, the manufactured home industry has experienced what happens with many other industries as well: lots of mergers and buy-outs. Soon, Brand X and its presumed competitor, Brand Y, are both owned by the same company. And then manufacturers start buying retail chains of dealerships and call them factory-direct stores.

These multiple-brand dealerships make it hard to tell from whom you are buying the home. How do you know the brand you just bought in Idaho isn't owned by a company in North Carolina, but maintains the same Idaho name? Soon, instead of 25 different manufacturing companies, there will be 20, then 15, then 10, and so on.

This is not free market economics but monopolization. It's like the big three auto makers that dominated US car manufacturing in the 20th century. Over time, only the largest and strongest survived (even though today, even those are struggling for survival), but the buyers aren't getting a better deal as a result. We fear this will continue to happen for some time to come with manufactured housing as well.

In fact, "factory-direct" does not really exist, except in name only. Here's why: A manufacturer can't sell homes to the public. Only a retailer can. That's why, when you call the factory and ask to buy a home from them, they refer you to a dealer. It is against the law for them to sell retail. They don't have a license to sell.

When one corporation owns both the factory and the retailer, it must maintain different entities. The dealership in fact buys the home from the factory and retails it to you at the most profit it can get. The factory-owned store has to keep books and buy homes from the factory just like any independent dealer. It is separate from the factory. We have found that dealerships that are owned by the corporation that owns the factory tend to ask the most money from you. Enter at your own risk. So much for "factory-direct savings."

So where are the good dealers with the good service? They are out there, but it can be tricky to find one. If you ask a dealership for references, guess what? They will give you only the good ones. That isn't going to help you. Call the state Consumer Affairs Office, the Better Business Bureau, and any other such office your particular state has. Most importantly, ask your neighbors who just bought a manufactured home what their experience was with the dealer, both before and after the contract was signed.

This may sound silly, but we suggest you also use your intuition. Instincts are often right and can tip you off to crooks. Don't be afraid to trust your intuition.

Truth in Advertising?

In general, most printed and televised advertising is used to pique your interest and get you to call or come in. That applies to manufactured home advertising as it does to most other forms. The advertiser just wants you to come in.

So far, so good. However, there are some companies that use very deceptive advertising to lure susceptible buyers into home-buying and financing nightmares. Let's look into some bad examples:

❏ "Divorce forces sale of home; will sacrifice huge equity."

Now you don't really believe someone would actually advertise his or her divorce in the classifieds, do you?

❏ "Missing… my wife. Please buy my new home before my aim gets better."

Yes, this ridiculous and offensive ad has been used.

❏ "Bob and Mary bought, Bob left and Mary lost. Assume $356 per month loan."

In this ad, there is neither Bob nor Mary. It's a dealer ad placed by a bored sales manager.

❏ "Abandoned home—take over payments."

Two things are wrong here. First, if a home is abandoned, the bank would take the house back; and second, if someone is moving out of their home, the bank would not let them bring in a second party to "take over payments."

Here's another cruel hoax for you to be wary of: A retailer advertises a 1,800 sq. ft. 4-bed, 2-bath double-wide for only $63,900. I'd be amazed if you could find a quality-built, correctly optioned home for such a low price. So how can a dealer advertise that price? By not including the cost of delivery and set-up. That's another $15,000, that you won't find out about until you're in the dealer's office, pen in hand, ready to sign off on the "deal." Don't sign that contract, but get full disclosures on all the homes you are considering.

There are many other forms of deceptive ads, but you can get a taste of them from just these few examples. You may be wondering if dealers really have sales and advertise honestly. Yes, sometimes they do. If you negotiate up from the dealer's cost of the home, you can consider that a sale.

If you are going to fall for ads like "one dollar over invoice," or "Special Purchase," or "Factory Sale," or "Big Discount on Sale Models," or "Close-Out Sale," then you will get taken at a "sale," as hundreds of other home buyers do. But you don't have to. Forget the ads and the gimmicks. Forget low-down-payment plans, "sales," and "factory-direct" pricing. Focus on the steps we will outline for you in the following chapters to get the lowest price on a new home and the maximum dollar on your trade.

Modern Sales Systems

Like so many people who have bought just about anything from anyone, we too have been romanced, confused, and charged just too much for goods and services at times.

King Solomon said it well: "There is nothing new under the sun." It's just packaged differently. Nothing could be more true when it comes to sales, salespeople, and dealership owners. Pushy, dishonest, promise-all salespeople and sales techniques are made, not born.

We have some harsh words for salespeople and, at the same time, much sympathy. There are many well-intentioned, care-a-lot people who make a living selling stuff. The problem may start during the Saturday morning sales meeting. General managers and sales managers (sales managers are the whipping boys of the general managers, and general managers get it from the owners) may be pressured by their bosses to motivate, intimidate, and plain old threaten salespeople to sell more. It does not matter the pecking order of the salespeople. The top dog is put under at least as much pressure as the rookie. Why do you think the salesperson of the year gets to be top dog? It's the one who makes the most profit for the dealership.

Quotas are set monthly and yearly for manufactured home salespeople, just as they are in the car showroom. Write-up goals are set, and salespeople often get "spiffed" for reaching the quota. How would you like to be a "write-up?" Sadly, in the sales world, change comes slowly —if at all.

How refreshing it is to find a salesperson who cares. One who actually asks you what you are looking for in a home, shows you what you want, and then helps you to achieve ownership in an honest way, not trying to control your every move and thought... This kind of salesperson does exist, and these people don't make any less profit for their employers—just in a more honest manner.

Think how pleasant it would be if a salesperson or a dealer would follow a simple set of rules: treat customers with respect and dignity, and deliver everything agreed upon. This isn't rocket science. Giving people everything they ordered isn't supposed to be that hard. Instead, far too many companies—and not just manufactured home dealers—make selling a complicated technique-oriented process, in which you, the "up" are an ignorant number. Confusion and control are what are in store for you—unless you are well prepared and take charge of the process for yourself.

This is probably the single largest purchase you will ever make. You need to know the details so you can remain in control of the process. Don't be led around by the nose.

Fig. 6.1. They don't all have to look like mini -mansions: This modern manufactured home by architect Rocio Romero is built on the same principles—but with a much more modern look The floor plan can be found on page 40.

Shopping For a Home

FINDING THE BEST home and paying a fair price for it can be a challenge. To succeed, you must put yourself in control of the situation. In the first part of this chapter, you'll find a "don't do it this way" scenario. Not to discourage you, but to learn from it. Once you've read the story and the evaluation that follows, you'll know how to go about it and keep yourself in control of the situation.

We'll be following the couple from Chapter 5 around as they go shopping for a new home. Because they're not properly prepared, they make some mistakes that finish up costing them extra time, money, and aggravation.

Travis owns his own business and Tara works as an assistant manager at a department store. They both deal with the public in their jobs and spend a good deal of time problem-solving for their customers, helping them get what they pay for.

After years of renting, they reached a decision to invest in a home and stop throwing money away as rent. The interest on their mortgage will be tax-deductible, and a home will give their children a better place to grow up. Travis's interest in manufactured homes was piqued when his neighbor put one on his property and was ready to move in after only three days. Both Travis and Tara were impressed with the way these homes had improved—not only in appearance, but also in the materials that were used in their construction. Additionally, the price was considerably less than it would have been for a site-built home of the same size and quality.

That Saturday is shopping day. At their first stop, they are greeted by a salesman wearing shorts, reeking of cigarette smoke. "Hi, how can we help you?" he asks.

"Well," says Travis, "we need a home."

The salesman responds, "They are all unlocked. Help yourself. I'll be in the office if you have any questions."

Travis and Tara begin walking from house to house, wandering, really, unsure of what they are looking at. Once they have seen all the homes, Tara likes several of them and needs to get some prices.

The salesman in the office quickly gives them some floor plans with some figures scribbled on them and tells them to have a nice day. Bewildered and somewhat turned around from all they had seen, they decide it's time to check out another dealership.

This time, the salesman seems a bit more helpful. He seems to have some energy and offers some useful information. "What is it you folks are looking for today?" he asks.

"We are in the market for a new house," Tara replies.

"Great! How many bedrooms do you need?" the salesman drools. "I've got this super house over here that's on sale and it's three bedrooms!"

Travis and Tara agree to see it, so off they go. "This home is a great buy and has many options," the salesman continues.

"What kind of options?" Travis asks.

"Well, I think the carpet is an upgrade, and this house has an optional ceiling fan."

Travis thinks the house is a bit plain and possibly too small. Tara agrees.

The salesman shoots a look in her direction and quickly suggests that for $58,900, they would be hard-pressed to find another home built with this quality and with this many extras.

"What makes your home better than all the others?" Travis asks.

"Everyone knows this brand is the Cadillac of manufactured homes, and our service is rated Number 1," responds the salesman.

"I see," Travis says quietly, figuring she missed something not knowing what "everyone" else seemed to know.

"Why don't we go in and write this one up. We have great financing here. On-the-spot approval," the salesman says, as he begins to walk toward the office.

Tara's face begins to crinkle, because she's feeling pressured. "Let's get out of here," she whispers to Travis.

"You got it," he says, and they leave.

Frustrated, and very disappointed that no one seems sincere or willing to spend time with them trying to find out what their needs are, they take a break.

"I don't get it," Tara says with a sigh. "This is turning out to be just like looking for a car."

"Yeah," Travis says. "We're talking about investing lots of money here. Why don't these places want to help us?"

Tired and suspicious, the two future homeowners decide to try one more dealership. This one has a 25-foot billboard along the expressway that reads, "Save thousands with factory-direct sales." The landscaping is immaculate, and there is an inviting sign on what appears to be the office; "Information and Welcome Center," it reads.

As Travis and Tara drive up to the Welcome Center, the salesman actually comes out and greets them at their car.

Now, this is more like it, Travis thinks. What service. The salesman is wearing a tie with slacks, and doesn't have a cigarette hanging out of his mouth.

"Welcome to Humongous Homes!" he says warmly." Is this your first visit?"

"Yes," Tara says.

"Well, wonderful! Come on in to our welcome center, so I can get some information from you." the salesman says, as he turns and almost runs back to the office.

Travis thinks this is certainly the place to buy. What enthusiasm!

Travis and Tara walk into the office, following the salesman back into his cubicle. It seems very inviting and warm. There isn't a desk, but rather a small round table with four chairs around it. There isn't even a door.

"May I offer you some coffee or soda?" the salesman asks. "By the way, my name is Dave," he says, extending his hand first to Travis and then to Tara.

"I'd like a diet soda," Tara says.

"I'll take one too, regular, though," Travis says. "I'm Travis, and this is my wife, Tara."

Handing them the cold soda cans, Dave says warmly, "So this is your first visit to Humongous Homes?"

"Yep," Travis responds.

"Well, you're in for a treat. We're different from most of your manufactured home dealers. Since we are owned by the factory, we can offer huge savings and great service. Why, we even own our own bank and insurance company. Let me show you."

Dave then pulls out from under his side of the table something that looks like a colorful flip chart, called *The Humongous Homes Story Book.*

Comfortable in their chairs, and sipping their sodas, Travis and Tara listen intently.

Dave goes on to explain each page of the storybook by reading script written on the back of the sheet. Twenty minutes and thirty pages later, Travis and Tara are thoroughly impressed. This company is on the ball. The salesman has taken the time to tell them the history of Humongous Homes and all the services that the company offers, not to mention how well-built the homes are. It's like one-stop shopping— the home, financing, insurance, the lot. Humongous Homes would even be the general contractor for Travis and Tara's site work.

Next, Dave asks, "In order for me to be of service to you, I need to ask you some income questions, so we know how much home you can afford. This way, I won't show you homes that are out of your reach. Besides, if you see too many homes, they just start to blend together anyway."

Travis and Tara agree.

"Tara," Dave asks," how much do you make a month?"

"About $1,600," Tara responds.

"Travis," Dave goes on, "how about you?"

"I bring in around $2,400. I'm self-employed, so it varies."

"Okay," Dave replies. "Let's do some figuring here and see what you can afford for a payment." He begins to punch these numbers into his calculator:

1,600 + 2,400 = 4,000

4,000 x 0.40 = $1,600.

(Note that Dave took 40% of $4,000 as the basis for his calculations instead of the 36% that are considered the maximum permissible. This got Travis and Tara into a higher payment.)

"Now, what are your monthly bills, not counting rent and utilities," Dave asks.

"Our car payment is $320, and we have three credit cards, on which we pay $260 a month," Tara replies.

"Great," says Dave and continues punching in numbers.

"$1,600 – $320 – $260 = $910 for monthly home payments. You folks have a good income, and according to my calculations, you can spend just about as much as you want." Dave continues, "Have you found any property yet?"

Travis replies, "No, not yet."

Dave says, "I can help you with that. We work exclusively with a realtor who can help you find land."

"You make it sound so easy," Tara says, relieved.

Dave knows he has some good buyers and continues to feed them.

"Travis and Tara, you are so much fun to work with. I can't tell you how refreshing it is to talk with people who know what they want."

Travis's chest puffs a little.

"By the way," Dave smiles, "for this month's promotion, we are giving away a free 42-inch flat-panel TV to go in your new living room!" His smile becomes more enthusiastic.

"Let's look at some other figures, so we can determine how much your land and improvements might cost." Out comes the calculator.

Tara expresses a concern: "What will our total payment be? How much are these homes? How much of a loan do we qualify for?"

"Let's finish our numbers and we will know. Of course, these are just estimates for now. Let's see," Dave mumbles. "Say you find land you like for $25,000. Then you need a foundation. That will cost about $5,000. You may need a well and a septic tank. That's probably $12,000. And $18,000 for a garage and driveway. Here's the figure I've come up with:

Land $25,000

Foundation . . . . $ 6,000

Well and septic tank $12,000

Garage and driveway $17,000

Site Development Total $60,000

"Wait. I'm confused, says Travis. We haven't even looked at a home yet." Dave's reply is smooth and sounds sincere. "I'm working backwards. That is, now that we know the estimated cost of your land and improvements, I can tell how much you have left for the home of your choice."

Here are the figures Dave uses to figure how much Travis and Tara can finance:

❏ $910 monthly payments

❏ 30-year term

❏ 5.5% APR

❏ Amount to finance: $160,211 (according to Dave's financial calculator, as used by all real estate and loan professionals)

"Well," Dave explains, "$160.211, minus $60,000 for improvements, leaves you $100,211 for a home. So let's go look at two or three in that price range.

"Great," says Travis. "Let's do it."

Dave doesn't even have to talk about a payment. This is perfect—for him at least.

The first home Dave shows Travis and Tara is 1,100 square feet with two bedrooms and two baths. "This is a neat cottage-style home and has a great little breakfast nook," Dave says proudly.

"What's the price on this one?" asks Travis.

I believe the range is $54–56,000, depending on the options," Dave smiles.

Tara says, "I would really like three bedrooms. And I'd like a little bigger kitchen. Can we see something bigger?"

"Sure," Dave says, ushering them to a small 3-bedroom model that is 1,228 square feet.

"This is better, but we still need a bigger kitchen," Tara says.

"Let's look at one more I think is the perfect home for you," Dave says, skipping out the front door.

The third house is also a 3-bedroom home, about 1,400 square feet. "This is you!" Dave says as he opens the door. "It's right within your budget, too—$84,800!"

Both Travis and Tara agree that the size is adequate and the price is right for what Dave has told them they can afford.

"This feels really cozy," Tara says.

"What do you think, Travis?" Dave asks.

"I think it will work perfectly," says Travis.

"Great! Let's go and start the paperwork and get you into financing," Dave says eagerly, as he leads them back to the Welcome Center and pulls out his purchase order book. Tara finally gets the nerve to ask again, "What will our monthly payment be?"

"It will be around $890 per month," Dave says.

"That's a big payment," Tara says.

"Don't worry," Dave says sympathetically "With your income, you can easily afford it."

Contracts and Finance Twists and Turns

Now Travis and Tara are seeing themselves in their new home. Dave has romanced them and seemed sincere. He even showed them a home in their price range that they liked. He seemed to know about finance, too. They think they have a good deal.

Dave begins to write all the required information on the purchase order: names, address, phone number, model of home, and stock number.

"Folks," he begins, "this is a lot model, so I won't need as much deposit to hold your home until financing is done, but I'm required to get at least 20% down."

"Twenty percent," Travis quips. "I don't have that much with me."

Dave replies, "You know, you are so well qualified, I'm going to talk to my sales manager to see if he would take less. I'll be right back."

"At least he's on our side," Tara says. A few moments later Dave returns with Buck, whom he introduces as the sales manager. Buck is an easy-to-talk-to guy and seems to know everyone in the area. Dave lets Buck sit in his chair.

"Hi, I'm Buck. Sounds like Dave here has helped you find the perfect home."

"Yes, he has," says Travis. "We just don't have the 20% down today."

"Tell you what," Buck says. "I'll go ahead and waive the 20% down and reduce it to 10% down. Sound okay?"

"Ten percent would be $8,480," Buck states, as though it took some real brain work to figure that one out.

"Okay," says Travis, "we can do that."

"Great. Let's get the paperwork done for you," grins Buck.

Dave continues to write on the purchase order: "Lot model or one like it."

"What does that mean?" asks Travis.

"Travis, quite honestly, it's for Humongous Homes' protection," Dave answers. "It takes 60 to 90 days to complete a land-home package like yours, and I'm not allowed to tie up a display model for that long. This allows us to sell the home and order you another just like it. Don't worry. The price won't change."

"Well, all right. Does it really take that long?"

"Sometimes. But we try to do land-home packages in 30 days," Dave says reassuringly, holding back a chuckle.

"What do you think our interest rate will be?" Tara inquires.

Dave's answer sounds reasonable. "It depends on your credit background. "Since Travis is self-employed, it will probably be a bit higher than usual. I'm sure it will be under 6 percent, though."

Travis doesn't realize that being self-employed does not disqualify someone from getting a competitive interest rate. Travis, concerned about his $8,480, says, "Can I get this back if we change our minds?"

"Oh, sure," Dave says. "Deposits are refundable if your credit is denied," leaving out that it doesn't apply if they just change their mind.

"That's what I was after," Travis says, relieved. "What's this $350 doc fee?"

Dave replies, "Our documentation fee is what you pay to cover the cost of getting you financed and all that other paperwork."

"Seems a bit high," Travis remarks.

"It's really not. Frankly, our costs are higher than you think."

Tara, curious about some of the small print below where they were supposed to sign, asks Dave, "What does it mean here, where it says 'tires and axles are returned to the dealer for recycling'?"

Dave smoothly replies, "We recycle tires and axles to save you, the customer, money. Neat, huh?"

"That makes sense," Tara agrees.

Both Travis and Tara are impressed. This is a really classy outfit. The salesman is genuinely concerned about them and very knowledgeable. No pressure, and easy financing, too. This is what we were looking for, they smile to each other.

After Dave is finished with the contract, he asks Travis and Tara to sign at the bottom. They do.

Next, Dave gets out a credit application for Travis and Tara to fill out. Surprisingly, it is only one page long and takes all of ten minutes to complete.

"Okay," Dave begins. "Next, I have to get this into finance. It shouldn't take but a few days. Why don't you two go take a look at your new home one more time."

"Sounds good," Travis says, putting an arm around Tara's shoulder as they go out the door.

"This turned out to be really easy," Tara says as they open the door to their future home. "But should we have looked at and priced more homes?" There are so many brands and so many other options. I mean, I really like this home, but I guess I'm just a little nervous.

"I'm feeling a little uneasy, too. I hear what you're saying," Travis responds.

"I guess we have to do this some time," Tara replies.

"Dave enters the home and says with a big smile, Come on out in front so I can get a picture of you two standing in front of your new home." Dave takes two pictures, one for Tara and Travis, and one for himself. "This will give you a reminder of how good this home fits you while we check on your financing. I'll call you in a few days."

Travis and Tara leave Humongous Homes with a picture of their new home and a promise of financing. Overall, they are very excited and glad at how things went. Their visit did cost them nearly $8,500, and the contract was a bit complicated, but they still feel happy.

Three days later, the phone rings. It is Dave; he says quietly, "I need for you and Tara to come in. We have to discuss your financing."

"All right. We'll be in this afternoon," Travis replies.

Dave has a serious look on his face as he meets Travis and Tara at the door. "Come back to my office, he says. Travis, Tara, we got your financing through, but it wasn't easy. Your payment is $1,000 a month."

Travis jumps. "What?"

"Just kidding," Dave grins. "We got your payment for $940 per month."

"That's better," Tara sighs with relief." It isn't the $890 that Dave had originally said, but at least it wasn't $1,000 a month. Dave has a good sense of humor, she decided.

"We ended up going with our company-owned bank because Travis's self-employment status presented some real difficulties to other finance companies," Dave says, showing some concern. "What we need to do now, he continues, is get land tied up for you and start the improvements. I'll call Lola. She can show you properties tonight if you like."

"Sounds great!" Travis and Tara say together, sounding excited.

After Travis and Tara find property and make an offer, Dave begins to report to them on bids for improvements, using the costs he had originally given, adding up to $35,000:

Foundation $6,000

Well. $6,000

Septic tank $6,000

Garage. $14,000

Driveway. $3,000

Dave knows these figures are higher than the actual cost of these improvements, but it increases his profit and gives him a bigger commission. He orders an appraisal of the project, as all lenders require an appraisal. Since it is a busy time of the year for appraisers, it takes almost three weeks.

Once the appraisal is finished, it is time to start the improvements on the property. The well is dug, followed by the septic tank installation. The contractor doing the foundation is booked, so he can't begin for a good two weeks. Finally he finishes the foundation and starts on the garage. During this time, Dave sells the home Travis and Tara put money down on (remember "lot home or one like it?"). Humongous Homes orders another one for Travis and Tara, but the factory is four weeks out, so another month is added to the process.

The garage is completed, and the house finally comes off the factory line, is delivered, and set on the foundation. Ten days later, the house is done, and Travis and Tara can finally close the deal.

As the credit manager is going over their loan papers, Travis notices the amount to finance was higher than he had thought.

He asks, "What happened to this figure? $160.211 package cost less $8,480 down payment equals $151,731 amount to finance'."

"Well," the loan officer begins, "we are adding your closing costs to your amount to finance. The closing costs are $4,400. Your monthly payment is $980."

"What?" Tara gasps. "We were told that it would be $940." She and Travis look at each other with consternation.

"We can do it," Travis says reassuringly. "Our house is delivered. The improvements are done. We can move in. It's okay. It'll be tough, but we can do it."

Travis signs first, and Tara signs with visible reluctance, and returns an uncertain smile to Dave's congratulations to the new home owners.

Analysis of the Story

This is a somewhat abbreviated story, but it demonstrates the experience many purchasers of manufactured homes go through. Let's see what Travis and Tara did wrong.

The biggest, most costly, mistake was not doing any preparatory homework. It cost them time and money, and it will stretch their income thin each and every month. I'm not saying they are stupid. They just trusted the wrong people.

First, before they even looked at any homes, they should have gone to a bank, a credit union, or a mortgage broker to get pre-qualified. Then they should have applied for a loan and waited for approval, so they would know the exact amount they could borrow, the down payment, the closing costs, the interest rate, and the terms of the loan.

Next, they should have sat down and determined what payment they were comfortable with, including taxes and insurance. Many lenders require that homeowners pay monthly on their taxes and insurance. Travis and Tara's payment ended up at $980. If you include a monthly tax and insurance payment of $400, their total will end up being around $1,380 a month.

Remember, even if you have less than perfect credit, don't go to the dealer for financing. Call a mortgage broker. You will get a better rate and won't put so much profit in a dealer's pocket.

Because Travis and Tara did not have a clear idea of the size of the home they needed, and failed to look at several, they settled for a home that they were unsure of. They took the word of a salesman who "hijacked" their home-buying process.

The contract was another stumbling block for Travis and Tara. Dave wrote "Lot model or one like it." This gave the dealer the right to sell the house to another buyer who could take delivery sooner. Obviously, you can tell from their story that Travis and Tara's home was indeed sold to someone else, and it cost them another month of waiting. It's a good thing their landlord was easy to get along with.

Thirty days is not realistic for a home-land package. Ninety days is much more like it, and it sometimes takes longer. Dave was a too optimistic.

Travis was smart to ask if he could get his deposit back. Humongous Homes was smarter (or rather, slicker) by having the contract preprinted with, "Deposit is fully refundable *if credit is denied*." What you have to realize is if a dealer gets financing approved at a lender for you, and you decide you don't like the terms, you lose your deposit. Don't sign that.

The next thing questioned was the doc fee: $350 for what? We believe this charge was swiped from the car dealers. A documentation fee will cover the cost to apply for title to your home. It varies, depending on what state you live in. We can't imagine that it would ever be more than $50. The dealer was cutting himself in for lots of profit here, too.

Next, Tara wondered what the tire and axle recycle clause meant. It's simple, really: You pay for the tires and the axles, and the dealer takes them back and sells them to someone else. What a deal!

After Travis and Tara filled out the credit application, Dave invited them out to see their home again and to get a picture. What better way to remind Travis and Tara of that house? This technique is a real lock-in for customers while they're waiting for finance approval. By taking two pictures, if Travis and Tara backed out of the deal, Dave still has a picture to hang on his wall for prospective customers to see.

The approval came back and Dave used a bit of shock therapy to soothe Travis and Tara into a higher payment. Read that part again: The payment went from $890 to $1,000, back to $940, but finished up at $980. What was going on?

Check carefully how long it took to do an appraisal and improvements. This part is not unusual, so be ready. The part that really hurt is when the dealer took advantage of the contract that Travis and Tara signed allowing the home to be sold to someone else. That took another month for delivery of the replacement home.

Also, Travis and Tara should have talked to some of their neighbors about their experience with their manufactured homes.

Finally, since Dave's knowledge of finance was minimal, he didn't mention closing costs and that they would be added to the total amount to finance, thus increasing the payment. Travis and Tara were so far along in the process, they felt obligated to sign off on the loan, but if you go back to the financial worksheet in Chapter 5, you'll see that their payment was more than their financial situation would allow.

As you can see, Dave was trained very well, probably by his company's "Sales Trainer." This is the guy who exclusively trains all new salespeople and indoctrinates them into a particular style of selling. In the case described above, the salesperson was taught just enough to be smooth and sound knowledgeable. His company showed him how to give only a limited amount of information to customers, and to participate in a lot of partial truths and "turnovers."

Look for these telltale control signs when you enter a dealership:

❏ All homes locked with signs on them that read something like, "To protect this home for its future owner, all homes are kept locked."

❏ The salesperson won't show you a home until you sit down in the office to get the pitch, that is, a flip-chart story book.

❏ The salesperson tries to qualify you, get your name, and asks if you have been elsewhere.

❏ The salesperson wants you to finance and insure with the dealership.

❏   A salesperson meets you at your car, welcomes you, then asks you to come into the office and doesn't wait for a reply and walks off.

Travis and Tara just endured and fell for a completely scripted situation. Sadly, this is all Dave was trained to do, and yes, as you can see, it usually works. He practices what his sales trainer has taught him: "You must make 28 demonstrations to get 7 write-ups."

Demonstrations? What is this, a car? These companies work on large numbers and quotas. Many pay their salespeople a monthly draw; it could be $1,500. When a salesperson sells a home, the commission is applied toward the accumulated draw. If it takes three months to close a land-home package and the salesperson has racked up a $4,500 draw, but his commission is only $1,500, then he or she is "in the hole" by $3,000. It's no wonder the annual turnover for salespeople is 80 to 90 percent. Humongous Homes, being as big as they are, will go through hundreds of salespeople a year. Smaller dealers can have similar training programs as well. There are a lot of consulting firms that do sales that way. You deserve better treatment.

Price

Unlike car dealers, manufactured home dealers are not required to display the MSRP (Manufacturer's Suggested Retail Price) in a window. The only way to find the exact cost a dealer paid for the home is to have exact costs for setup and delivery (and everything it entails). Plus, you would need to know the holdback the dealer gets from the manufacturer. It is unlikely you will be able to gather all these figures. But perhaps you can come close by using the example below and doing some homework.

Many retailers use PACs. PAC is a term used to describe a cost of setting up a home. These prices will vary from state to state and from dealer to dealer. If you can talk the retailer into giving you a list of all the subcontractors they use to complete the set-up of your home, you can call them and get their bids.

Dealer invoice is what the dealership paid the factory for the home. Actually that's not quite true: The invoice has kickbacks, or "VIP-money," built into it. These kickbacks are paid to the dealership once a year and are incentives for them to sell homes. They can be anywhere from 2% to 11% of the price per home—and sometimes even more. Don't plan on the dealer ever giving up this money, even though it is really your money. The invoice on a manufactured home will have the base cost to the dealer, the cost of the options, and the freight. From time to time, a rebate will appear, but you will never know. Because of this holdback money, and depending on the deal the retailer negotiates with the manufacturer, different dealers can end up paying different prices for the same home.

Table 6.1 shows typical costs for set-up of single-, double-, and triple-wide manufactured homes. The list is not exhaustive, but it covers the basics for within 100 miles from the dealership.

As you can see, it is a huge undertaking to deliver and set up a manufactured home. By the time all is said and done, there will have been six to eight subcontractors working on your home. Use this list as a base, not as exact figures. Because there's no MSRP posted on the home, we've devised this table as an approximate guide that will get you close to what the dealer paid for the home.

The following steps show you how you go about getting a handle on the dealer's price to help you establish a fair price to pay.

1. Ask the dealer for his base price. If he won't give you one, walk out.

2. Ask what the base price includes (delivery and setup, freight, tape and texture, etc.). Generally the base price will include delivery to your site, but options will be extra.

3. Deduct from the base price the appropriate PAC. (Base that number on the figures in Table 7.1)

Table 7.1. Typical manufactured home set-up costs

	Single-wide	Double-wide	Triple-wide
Freight from factory	$550	$950	$1,500
Set-up and finish work	$1,500	$3,000	$4,500
Carpet laying	$0	$600	$800
House cleaning	$200	$300	$400
Tape and texture close-up	$800	$1,800	$2,500
Total PAC	**$3,050**	**$6,650**	**$9,700**

Example:

Dealer base price (double-wide): $90,000

Less PAC . . . . −$6,650

Home price $83,350

Of the $83,350 remaining, a certain percentage is profit, and the balance is the dealer invoice. Start high. Figure 23% of that is profit. This isn't always true, because some dealers sell at a lower profit margin and make a living on kickbacks.

Profit: 23% of $83,350 = ... $19,170

Dealer cost: $83,350– $19,170 = ... $64,180

Dealer invoice is $64,180. His kickback will be between $1,000 and $4,000, so the home actually cost the dealer between $60,180 and $63,180. Now you know something that they don't like you to know, and you can use it to negotiate the price down to a figure that's fair on you, leaving the dealer no more than their job is worth, perhaps $2,000 or at most $3,000 more than their cost, not that absurd 20-odd percent figure they'd like you to sign off on.

Shop Around

Who is going to give you the best deal? To find out, it pays to shop around. Put on your walking shoes; it's the most profitable homework you'll ever do. If possible, visit at least three different dealers who sell the brand you're interested in. At the first stop, sit down with a salesman and spec out a house with the options and upgrades you would like. Have them give you a total delivered and set-up price. Then request a copy of the option sheet. Tell the salesperson you need to study everything at home. If he or she objects, say that's what you do before you buy anything. If the dealership won't part with an option sheet, say good-bye and walk out.

Take the list you finally do get to two other dealers and have them give you a price on the exact same house. Tell the salesperson that you are shopping, and *do not reveal* the base prices you were quoted by the other dealers. Don't forget to get their base price. Also, remember to take copies for yourself, so an unscrupulous dealer doesn't do some adding and subtracting on the options sheet. Leave that original one in the car.

So, you're thinking, why can't I just call and get the dealer's base price? Because you will get low-balled on the phone every time, to get you to come and see them in person.

What is a fair profit for a dealer to make on the sale of a home? $5,000, $10,000, $15,000? Or how about $2,000 or $3,000? Here are some typical markups on single-, double-, and tripe-wide homes for you to consider during your calculations:

Single-wide. 18–23%

Double-wide 19–24%

Triple-wide 20–26%

The profit will be less on a single-wide than on a triple-wide, with the double-wide somewhere in between. We have seen profit on the sale of a triple section home push $35,000. Ouch!

Your goal should be to find the least amount of profit a dealership will take, using the following techniques:

❑ Studying the specs on a house, comparing apples to apples.

❑ Negotiation.

❑ Beating the sales techniques (Remember: he who speaks first loses).

8 Finding a Home for Your Home

TO DECIDE whether to put your home in a manufactured home community or on your own land, there are several factors to consider. These include your financial situation, your own personal goals, how much maintenance you want to deal with, and your age. To decide what is best for you, you need what's called a "cost-benefit analysis."

Comparing Pros and Cons

Let's first look at financial condition. Here's a chart to compare the costs as well as the advantages and disadvantages of the two available options, based on a modest single-wide:

1. Home on Own Land

Home	$60,000
Land	$25,000
Improvements	$20,000
Miscellaneous	$ 5,000
Total cost.	**$110,000**

And here's how that works out in terms of your monthly payment:

Total cost	$110,000
Less down payment (10%)	−$11,000
Amount to finance:	$99,000
Principal and interest (at 4.5%, 30 years)	$502
Monthly taxes and insurance	$300
Total monthly payment.	**$802**

2. Home, Renting Space:

Home	$60,000
Improvements required by landlord:	$2,000
Less 5% down payment on the house	−$3,000
Amount to finance.	**$59,000**

And here's how this option works out in monthly cost:

Principal and interest (at 5.5%, 25 years).	$362
Insurance	$60
Space rent.	$450
Total monthly payment.	**$872**

Let's look at the pros and cons of the two ways of placing the home.

Home on Own Land

Pros:

1. Your home won't depreciate (instead, it'll probably appreciate in value if it's placed on a foundation).

2. The whole package will be yours once the mortgage is paid up.

3. You can do what you want on your land as far as improvements —within state and local zoning laws.

4 You'll have privacy and "elbow room."

Cons:

None that we can think of.

Home, Renting Space

Pros:

1. Especially in 55-and-over communities, probably little or no yard work or outside maintenance.

2. Maybe a gated community with its own security.

3. You can move your home relatively easily.

Cons:

1. Your home's value is more likely to depreciate than to appreciate.

2. If you decide to move, it will be costly and hard on your home.

3. You have to comply with the owner's rules and covenants.

4. The space rent can, and probably will, go up.

5. Sometimes, community management can be very grouchy and hard to deal with.

6. Any improvements you make and spend money on usually stay there if you move.

7. Communities are becoming increasingly picky on the age of homes they allow.

Manufactured Home Communities

That's what they like to be called, rather than "trailer park." The following is a generic list of guidelines and rules you may encounter if you place your home in a manufactured home community. This list is, of course, not exhaustive; however, it will give you an idea of what is allowed and tells you restrictions communities are likely to place on you. The rules of the community you choose may be different in some details, so it will behoove you to read them carefully to make sure a rented space is for you. Pay special attention to rules number 27 and 28.

Number 27 allows the management or owner to approve or disapprove of a potential buyer, should you ever decide to sell your home. Do not accept this. A community owner probably does this to reject all potential buyers that make good offers on your house. He will then make a lowball offer on your house, and you have to sell to him at the price he offers, while he can then resell it at a high profit.

Number 28 is also very bad, because worded this way, "the sky is the limit." Make sure there is something in writing that is specific about by how much rent can be raised, and in what time frame. The way it is phrased here is too vague.

If these guidelines and rules don't correspond with how you envision your lifestyle, a manufactured housing community will not be a good place for your home and your family.

Typical Community Guidelines

Guidelines are standards for new home installations and for improvements made by existing tenants at resale or replacement.

1. Fences:	New fences may be a maximum of 36 inches high and enclose only the rear one third of the lot. Fences may be chain link with a top rail, wood, or wood-look vinyl. Wood fences can be solid or picket type. All fences should have at least one access gate. Upon sale and/or occupancy change of existing homes, all front yard fencing must be removed and fences higher than 36 inches should be removed or reduced to 36 inches.
2. Deck and Steps:	Deck and steps must be skirted to match home skirting. Manufactured steps must be installed at all doorways. Railings are required. All wood should be painted or stained to match the color of the home. Color-coordinated outdoor carpeting is

encouraged. Temporary steps must be removed within 60 days of occupancy.

3. Sheds:
Sheds may be wood or metal but must match the home in color. No more than two sheds are allowed. Sheds must be placed at the rear of the driveway.

4. Storage:
All RVs, boats, and extra vehicles must be stored in the storage area, not at the home site. If the storage area is full, items must be stored off-site.

5. Awnings:
Newly installed homes must have awnings installed within 90 days. A minimum 10 ft. x 40 ft. patio awning and all entry doors must have an awning cover. If the space has a side driveway, parallel to the home, a driveway awning will be required. Awnings may be required on existing homes at sale and/or occupancy change.

6. Antennas:
Antennas or satellite dishes must be approved in writing. They may be located on the roof away from the street or at the rear of the home out of sight. Dishes must be 18 inches or smaller.

7. Landscaping:
The entire lot must be landscaped within 90 days of move-in. Drought resistant landscaping is highly recommended. Landscaping must include some plants. Small vegetable gardens may be planted at the rear of the home site, but should not be visible from the street.

Typical Community Rules

The following rules are for the protection and welfare of the tenants and visitors to this community. Any violation of the rules will be sufficient to commence legal eviction proceedings to have the tenant and the home removed from the community. The management reserves the right to alter any of the following rules upon ninety (90) days written notice.

1. Tenant and any occupant must register and be listed at the community manager's office prior to moving the home into place.

2. The home must be set in place by a company approved by the management and placed on the lot only as specified by management within thirty (30) days of executing the rental agreement.

3. All homes will be inspected by management prior to placement in the community. Management will prohibit placement of any home which, in management's sole discretion, fails to meet the minimum community requirements or established National Manufactured Housing Standards. Tenant's home shall be in good repair and must bear a current annual license or State identification number.

4. Skirting is required to be installed within sixty (60) days after the home is placed on the lot. Removable tongues and hitches shall be taken off prior to skirting. Permitted skirting materials are manufactured metal skirting that matches the home, wood if the home is wood, or masonry. Vents must be installed for safety.

5. Each space is provided with a driveway for parking. Tenant may not alter driveway or walkways without prior approval of the manager. Any approved concrete added by the Tenant shall be done to professional standards.

6. Each home space must be identified by a space number. Space numbers of 3 inches should be affixed to each home.

7. All utility hookup connections from the existing electrical, water, sewer, telephone, and gas lines, if any, must comply with local and state regulations, and any wiring, plumbing, or other hookup costs whatsoever, are the responsibility of the tenant. Electrical connections must be made by a licensed electrician.

8. All tenants' garbage, trash, or refuse shall be kept in covered metal or plastic containers, which must be periodically cleaned and free from any obnoxious odor and/or insects, and must be placed in or at the rear of the tenant's home in an inconspicuous place or at the place designated by management.

9. The tenant shall keep and maintain the premises in a neat, clean, and orderly condition and free of debris. The tenant shall also wa-

ter, mow, and trim the tenant's lawn and care for any shrubbery and perform ice and snow removal when needed. If the tenant fails to do any of the above, the management will order the work completed to community standards and all costs of such work will be charged to the tenant; these costs will be treated as additional rent and payable by the first of the following month. Tenant will receive an itemized billing of such charges when incurred.

10. Awning, patio enclosure, any construction, or other improvements on the lot must be approved in writing by the management. Approval shall only be granted after plans or proper descriptions have been submitted to the management. All construction and improvements shall meet all applicable state and local codes.

11. Any requests for improvements, alterations, fencing, landscaping, gardening, planting of shrubs, flowers, trees, or other exterior improvements must be submitted in writing and will be allowed only with the management's prior written approval. The tenant shall not make any penetrations into the ground, such as placing posts, stakes, etc., that might interfere with underground utilities, without the management's prior written approval. The height of any extensions that exceed four (4) feet above the tenant's home must be approved in writing by the management. Any improvements, the removal of which would significantly damage the landscape of the home lot, shall not be removed by the tenant when vacating the community. If the tenant removed improvements when vacating, the tenant shall leave the lot in substantially the same condition as, or better than, upon taking possession.

12. Vehicular traffic within the community shall not exceed ten (10) miles per hour and shall stop to give pedestrians the right of way. Tenants or guests of tenants are not to walk through or trespass upon other lots or use vacant lots for any purpose.

13. Vehicles not in regular use, pickups larger than ¾ ton, boats, boat trailers, campers, trailers, snowmobiles, and other recreational vehicles may not be stored in the community except in a separate storage area, if available. Inoperative vehicles and unlicenced vehicles must be stored outside the community.

14. Off-street parking is provided at the tenant's home space. Tenant shall not park any vehicles in the community's streets except for loading or unloading, unless special arrangements are made with the management. Visitors' cars may be parked only in front of the tenant's space for a short period of time.

15. Wading pools, swings, slides, and other similar types of equipment shall not be permitted on lawns, unless the tenant obtains prior approval in writing from the management.

16. Space under and around the tenant's home must be kept clean and sanitary at all times, and nothing shall be stored under the home until the home has been properly skirted and the type of storage has been approved by the management. Other outside storage is not allowed except in a storage shed approved in writing by the management as to type, color, manufacturer, and location. Standard yard and patio furniture, barbecue equipment, and approved lighting equipment are permitted in the tenant's space and must be kept in good condition. No fuel, oil, or other materials of a combustible nature shall be stored under or near the home, or anywhere in the community, if it is considered a danger to others. The hanging of clothes on an outside clothesline is allowed only at the rear of the space. A small amount of cut and neatly stored fire wood may be kept at the space.

17. Trespassing, loud or disturbing noises, the use of motorcycles or motor bikes within the community, obnoxious odors, and/or other disturbances or conduct by a tenant or his guests that is offensive or violates other tenants' or management's right to quiet and peaceful enjoyment of the community will not be tolerated and subject the tenant to eviction from the community.

18. The tenant agrees NOT to keep pets on or within the community unless otherwise approved in writing by the management. If small pets are permitted, they must measure less than 18 inches high at the shoulders, fully grown, and must be kept within the tenant's home. The tenant must register such pets with the management and must show proof of immunization for any pet subject to rabies. Dogs or cats must be neutered. Any pet that becomes a problem for

any tenant or management shall be removed from the community immediately by the tenant at the request of the management. Pets other than those owned by tenants will not be permitted on the community premises. Cages or dog houses are not permitted outside the home. Pets outside the home must be on a leash at all times. This paragraph does not imply that pets will be allowed.

19. Homes must be periodically washed and/or painted as may be necessary to maintain an attractive appearance. It shall be done in such a manner so as not to cause damage or be a nuisance to the adjoining residents.

20. Residents must provide heat tapes to protect waterlines from freezing. These tapes must be connected to the home's utilities at the time of the initial hook-up. Residents will be held responsible for the expense to repair frozen water lines on the resident's lot. The tenant shall notify the management of any water hydrant problems immediately.

21. The resident's home or lot must not be used for any business or commercial operation, including the sale of trailers, vehicles, or other type of merchandise or by providing a service to members of the public at the tenant's home. If tenants desire to sell their home, they must first advise the management of your intent. "For sale" signs must be approved by the community management in advance and situated next to the home or in a window. Contact the community management for any assistance they may be able to provide.

22. All vehicles must conform to local laws regarding emissions and repairs. Corrective action must be made immediately when requested by the management. Vehicles dripping oil or gas must be repaired in a timely manner and drip spots on parking surfaces must be cleaned by the resident. Repairs, tune-ups, oil changes, or overhauling of motor vehicles are not permitted in the community.

23. A recreation building, storage area, and other facilities, if furnished, are for the tenant's enjoyment and use. The tenant must abide by the rules and regulations posted by the management at

the respective facilities. All persons using the community facilities do so at their own risk.

24. Solicitors, vendors, peddlers, and other similar business activities are considered an intrusion, and are not permitted in the community. Necessary delivery men who are authorized by management may have access to the community.

25. Violations of any law or ordinance of the city, county, state, or federal government will not be tolerated and are sufficient reason for eviction. Acts which could place the management or owner of these premises in violation of a law or ordinance of the city, county, state, or federal governments will not be permitted. The tenant shall pay all taxes on his home and improvements due by reason of any federal, state, county, or municipal law.

26. The management reserves the right of access to the tenant's lot at all times for the purposes of inspection or maintenance of utilities and to temporarily move tenant's home for repairs of any of the community's facilities.

27. The management reserves the right to approve or disapprove of any potential buyer the tenant may wish to sell his/her home to.

28. The management reserved the right to adjust rent according to the market condition.

Moving Your Manufactured Home

Even if you are a single-wide buyer, it is important to realize that these homes aren't your grandma's trailer any more. Please don't think you can move a modern manufactured home overnight to a different location. A 14 x 70 ft. single-wide entails much more to move than they used to—not to mention the expense. Let us give you an idea of cost here:

Tires and axles charge $300

Tear-down of skirting, awnings $600

Freight to new site $1,000

New set-up $1,500

Re-skirt $800

Tape and texture repair $700

Total **$4,900**

Surprising, isn't it? If you ever have to move, it may be more cost-effective to plan on selling your home right where it sits, unless you have family and friends who can do this work for you.

Trading Houses

Let's talk about trades. Say you've lived in a 1998 single-wide and now it's time to get into something a bit nicer and newer. Watch out: here's what can happen and how to protect yourself.

Many dealerships don't post the prices of their model homes. Rather, the salesperson will give you ranges of cost that depend on how the house is equipped. One of the first things a salesman will ask you is if you have a trade. Don't fall for this: that way he will know if he has to inflate the price of the new home to accommodate your trade. This is most common, but there are a few dealers who will deduct what you want for your trade from their retail price, which is inflated anyway.

Here is the best thing you can do if you have a trade. If you own it free and clear, you're in a better position than most. First, get a wholesale trailer trader to give an actual cash-value appraisal of your home. Try to get at least two appraisals. Be ready: older manufactured homes do not have as much value as you may think. Wholesale, your 20-year-old single-wide is probably worth only about $4,500 if it is in good condition. $4,500 is what the wholesaler will pay you; then, in turn, he will turn around and sell it at retail for around $8,000.

These figures can vary for different parts of the country, of course. Next, you can try to sell your home yourself. Advertise in the paper or on a community website, such as *Craigslist.org*. Be prepared to dicker a little. Make whoever buys your house responsible for having it moved; you have enough to deal with already.

Of course, the most hassle-free way to sell your house is to let the wholesaler buy it. No muss, no fuss. You may not make quite as much as you would like, but it's the quickest way.

If you owe money on your home and want to trade it in, you need to find out whether your home is worth more than you owe. The way to determine the value of your house is to have the wholesale trailer trader give you a written bid. He will use a Blue Book similar to what's used for determining the value of used cars. Alternately, you can simply look in your neighborhood or town to see what comparable homes are selling for. At this point, if you are "upside-down" (meaning you owe the bank more than the home is worth), you must make a decision: Stay in your home a few more years or trade it in at a dealership and add the balance of what you owe to the new loan. Doesn't it sound like we're trading a car here? If you're smart, you'll try to sell your home first—hopefully for a few thousand more than you owe, if you can't stay put until the situation changes. Don't rush it, because that will cost you dearly.

A favorite ploy of many dealers is to advertise massive trade-in allowances for your trade. But when you check further, you will find that the promotion applies only to non-advertised homes. This is because you already know the price of their advertised homes, so they can't increase their price to "allow" for what you want for your trade. The dealer will make you order a home so he can adjust the selling price.

If you must trade in your home, and you own it free and clear, follow the steps given in Chapter 6 to figure the approximate dealer cost of the new home (based on a final delivered and set-up cost with the options you want). Once a negotiated price is reached, *only then* tell the salesperson that you have a trade.

Have the dealer look at your trade and tell you what they will give for it. If it is not what the trader has quoted you, tell them you have had the house appraised at a certain price and that is what you want for it. The salesperson may turn green at this point and bring in his sales manager, but if you stick to your guns, you'll win, because they'll want to make that sale, even if they can't make the kind of killing they had hoped to make.

Land Improvements

Owning your own property can be the most satisfying and secure feeling you can have. It does take some work, though. Consider where you live before you buy. People who live where it snows can run into city and county restrictions that prohibit manufactured homes. In many cases, the federal regulation overrides the state or local restriction. It can take a visit to the City Attorney or to a Planning and Zoning committee meeting, so be prepared.

As manufactured homes have changed, so have many zoning laws. In many places, you may now place a double- or triple-wide, as long as it is installed on a poured concrete foundation, with sidewalks, and whatever else the city or county requires. You may need an 80-lb. roof load for snow or some type of retaining wall somewhere on your property.

Foundation

People use the word "foundation" a bit loosely, so let's clarify what it really is. A foundation is a permanent support for the home, made of concrete, poured from a cement truck in between form boards. The size of the footers and stem walls will vary depending on the building codes in your area and the manufacturer's specifications. There will be poured or pre-formed pads placed every so many feet under the I-beams and the marriage line of the home, depending on the manufacturer's requirements. Refer to Figs. 8.1through 8.4; what you see there are photos and technical drawings of typical solid-perimeter foundations for double- and triple-wide homes.

There seems to be some confusion between the above description of a foundation and what is called a "block foundation." It is built up of cinder blocks. Despite the name, it's not really a foundation at all but merely a (temporary) support. Unlike a solid, poured concrete foundation, the perimeter of the home does not rest on the block foundation. It's just the T-frame that is supported the way it would be supported by the axles and wheels of a trailer.

Manufactured homes are designed to be supported by cinder block or jack stands solely under the length of the I-beam and the marriage line. The solid perimeter foundation was developed to satisfy banks to achieve real estate status and therefore qualify for financing. It also brings the level of the home down closer to the ground, giving it a more residential appearance. In addition, the weight of the home is evenly distributed over the walls of the foundation and throughout the support system under the entire home, so there will be less settlement—and it won't get blown away in a storm.

Even with cinder block foundations it is possible to achieve the house look, and it is a bit cheaper. You get the house look by hiding the gap under the house by means of a cinder block wall, instead of traditional skirting.

There are some circumstances where it's OK to save yourself the cost of a poured concrete foundation, e.g. if the home is to be used as a weekend getaway, or as a temporary dwelling. In this case, it is important to correctly "grade" the soil under the home for water run-off. You don't want water to settle under the house, which can be a health hazard. This can be achieved in one of two ways: either make sure the center of the

Above and below: Figs. 8.2 and 8.3. Typical poured concrete solid-perimeter foundations for double-wide and triple-wide homes.

home sits on higher ground, sloping down toward the perimeter (see Fig. 8.5), or have the home sit on a slope, preferably sloping down toward the back of the house. Either way, it is generally recommended to place 6-mil (i.e. 0.006 in. thick) polyethylene sheeting under the home. In addition, it will be wise to dig a 1 ft. x 1 ft. or larger trench around the home, filled with gravel for drainage.

For a permanent dwelling, in the long run, it will be wiser to spend the extra money and go with the poured foundation. Resale value will be better, and there will probably be less settling in the house, and con-

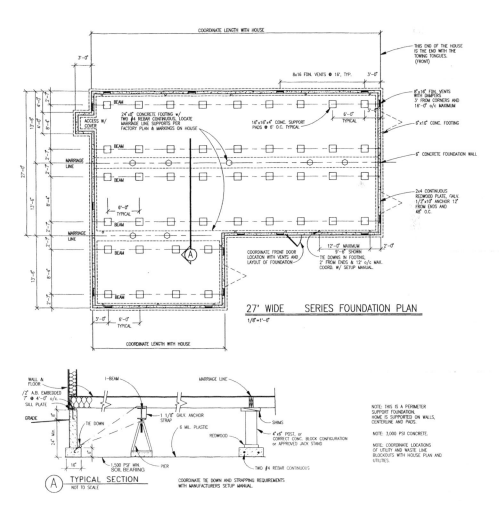

Fig. 8.4. Typical perimeter foundation plan drawing for a triple-wide.

sequently not as much need for texture repair in the interior, especially with large double- and triple-section homes.

One kind of foundation you *don't* need is what's called a "slab foundation." That's a large concrete pad the size of your home. Don't let some contractor or salesperson talk you into that kind of foundation: It is more expensive, wasteful (lots of unnecessary concrete will get poured for it), and it is neither something the building codes require nor what the manufacturers recommend for manufactured homes.

Well and Septic Tank

Concerning wells, discuss this issue with a well driller. He can tell you how deep you may need to drill and how many horse power or KW are required for pumping, depending on your needs. Also the size and location of your septic tank should be discussed with an expert.

Garage and Other Improvements

The next big improvement is a garage. You may attach it to the house or have it free-standing. Get bids on both. It's better to have it a bit larger than you think you need. How many cars do you want to store? Do you need extra room for a workbench? Make sure the pitch of the roof matches that of the house, and if the garage isn't larger than a two-car,

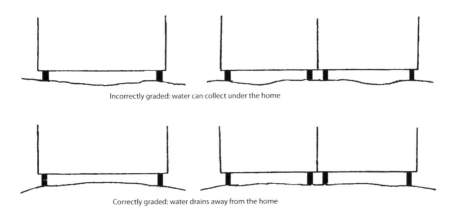

Incorrectly graded: water can collect under the home

Correctly graded: water drains away from the home

Fig. 8. 5. Soil grading for a manufactured home placed on cinder block piers (i.e., without solid perimeter foundation).

consider building the pitch of the roof so snow and rain will slide to the sides of the garage, rather than to the front. Think about any other utility buildings you may need as well.

Landscaping, fences, driveways, gravel, how to bring electric power into the site, hooking up city sewer and water, and any other item you may need should be discussed with specialized contractors familiar with local building codes and zoning rules.

Basements

Honestly, a basement is not a good financial proposition. Our experience with basements is that they are very expensive. Expect to pay at least $70,000 for a 28 x 60 foot daylight basement with 9-foot walls. The other reasons we do not recommend going this route are that many manufacturers won't build the stairwell hole into the floor and manufactured homes do not lend their floor plans to an interior stairway. There are more reasons besides cost and location of the stairway, but let us end here and just suggest you buy a larger home instead.

Fig. 8.6. A separate two-car garage with roof pitch sloping to the sides. This is smarter than sloping to front and rear, providing rainwater drainage away from the entrance. Of course if you want to save money, you could go for a carport instead and convert it to an enclosed garage later.

9

Finding the Best Home

O F COURSE, we have our personal opinions on this matter, and so does everybody else. You will need to do your own research to learn which home will be the best for your money, based on what you know about what you can afford. (You've already gone to a bank or mortgage broker to get qualified for a loan, right?)

You can use the following pages as a checklist to follow as you visit manufactured home dealerships. It is important to sit down and think about which options and upgrades you really need and which ones you may be prepared to do without.

There are certain options we will address that we believe to be essential, followed by some that you should consider, and finally, some options to avoid.

Do not allow the salesman to talk you into a particular option because it's a good buy "only from the factory." This is usually not true. There are certain items that you have to order from the manufacturer,

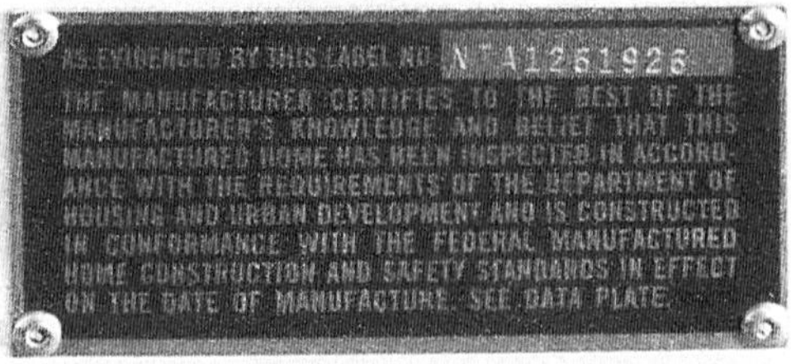

MHI photo

Fig. 9.1. The HUD tag. Any manufactured home must have a tag like this to certify that it meets the HUD code requirements. It is the only federal code for any type of home, assuring a certain minimum quality is met.

but many other ones are less expensive when purchased at your local hardware store and can be easily installed by you yourself. In general, dealerships will not mark up options from the factory and don't care which ones you choose. Their money is made by the profit from the sale of the house. Here's how it works:

The manufacturer of the home doesn't offer the color or quality of carpet you want, so you have to live with the 10 or so choices from the dealer's sample board, right?

Wrong.

First, find out how many square yards of carpet are used in the house. Then go to a carpet store and get a quote on the type and color you want. Get at least 52-ounce carpet and 6- or 7-lb. pad. Go back to the dealer and ask for the factory credit on the carpet. Unfortunately, that credit won't be as much as the dealer paid, but it is better than nothing. With the price of a good carpet in hand, including installation, simply add it to the price of the house. Then on the contract to purchase, simply add: "Humongous Homes to pay Cal's Carpet House up to $2,000" (or whatever is the price of the carpet). This concept can work with many different options in your house, such as valances, mini-blinds, appliances, and light fixtures.

Left: Fig. 9.2. 12-inch wide eaves like these give a more residential look to the house.

Below: Fig. 9.3. An outside "bib" (hose connection) is an important option.

Recommended Factory Options

Here is a list of options that we recommend to have installed at the factory, unless you are a heck of a good do-it-yourselver:

Exterior

1. Outside water faucets — at least two. Put one on each end of the house or put one each near the front and back doors, depending on the floor plan and how you set your house on the site.

2. Widest eaves (roof overhangs) available. Many manufacturers will put 12-inch eaves standard on the ends and sides of their houses, though they will make you pay for it. Buy it. Wide eaves keep the weather off your siding and give your home a better appearance.

3. Air conditioner-ready. This gives the home an extra junction box under the house. This option is necessary if you are going to have an air conditioner installed. It also gives you a thermostat that allows you to switch from the furnace to the air conditioner.

4. Consider a meter base; if you are going to have underground power, this option puts an electric meter base on the side of your house.

5. Heavy insulation package. We use this term to cover whatever the particular manufacturer offers in the way of additional insulation, such as 2 x 6 walls, 2 x 6 floors, vinyl-clad dual-pane widows, R-33 insulation in the ceiling, R-19 in the walls, and R-33 in the floor. It doesn't matter what part of the country you live in, you need to hold in heat or cool air.

6. 36-inch wide steel or metal-clad front door. It should be an "in-swing door."

7. Asphalt or fiberglass 3-tab shingles.

8. Vinyl or hardboard siding. (Vinyl siding is low-maintenance, but when it comes to achieving a quality appearance and ecological consciousness, painted hardboard siding is preferable.)

Kitchen

1. Solid wood cabinets. Don't try to save money on cabinets. Specify solid wood. Anything else will fall apart in a short time.

2. Plumbing for ice maker. If you have a refrigerator that has an ice maker, you need to have the plumbing built into the floor.

3. Garbage disposal. If you want a garbage disposal, have the factory install it. We have had to go in after the fact to install one, and it was a costly project.

4. Adjustable shelves. These are generally standard with solid wood cabinetry, but check first. You'll really need them.

5. Tile backsplashes. No wood or laminate, because it will crack, warp, and deteriorate when it gets wet.

6. Metal single-lever faucets and metal shut-off valves under the sink. It is important to have this in the kitchen for ease of operation. Most of the time, manufacturers will install a decent brand of faucet. Remember, no plastic.

7. Two fluorescent lights.

Left: Fig. 9.4. Recessed entry with 36-inch insulated steel-clad inswing door.

Below: Fig. 9.5. Double stainless steel kitchen sink with single-lever metal faucet.

8. Overhead lights in the pantry. Some manufacturers cut costs by not putting lights where they are really needed.

Utility Room

2. Cabinets above the washer and dryer area. Don't settle for just a shelf; you need as much enclosed storage as you can get.

3. Minimum 40-gallon water heater (50-gallon is preferable). Get a gas water heater, if possible, for economical operation. Alternately, you may be able to upgrade to a (more efficient) tankless water heater. And for a larger home, it's more efficient to have separate water heaters for both ends of the home.

4. No polybutylene plumbing. Many manufacturers use a high grade of plastic (PVC), which works fine. However, PCVC is even better.

Left: Fig. 9.6. One-piece fiberglass shower enclosure with glass sliding doors.

Below: Fig. 9.7. Deep utility sink with metal faucet and tile backsplash. Reject plastic.

All Bathrooms

1. Metal faucets and metal shut-off valves under the wash basin and the toilet tank. Remember, no plastic fixtures.

2. Porcelain or vitreous china washbasins. Plastic basins tend to melt when a curling iron is near. Vitreous china is becoming more common in manufactured homes. It is the same material that the toilet is made of.

3. Large mirror over washbasins with a sconce lights on both sides. You'll need the extra light, and side-light is better than overhead.

4. Fiberglass one-piece tub/shower combo. Porcelain and steel tubs are generally not available in manufactured homes. Fiberglass can be fine, but avoid plastic tubs and plastic 2-piece shower stalls or tub/shower combinations. The plastic ones are hard to keep clean and tend to crack.

5. Tile backsplashes.

6. If extra storage, such as a linen closet, is offered, get it. It'll come in very handy.

All Bedrooms

1. Overhead ceiling light. Even with bedside lights, you still need a central light with a switch next to the door. No plastic light covers.

2. Windows appropriately placed to allow for a headboard. Make sure windows are not "floating" in the middle of a wall.

3. Closets. Make sure they are big enough for you. Have them enlarged if they are too small.

4. Locking door knobs.

5. Wiring for a ceiling fan.

Dining Room

1. Sheet vinyl or (real) hardwood flooring, certainly if you have kids.

2. Wiring for a ceiling fan.

Living Room, Family Room

1. Windows appropriately located, depending on placement of your furniture.

2. Overhead ceiling lights.

3. Wiring for a ceiling fan.

Entry Way

1. Sheet vinyl or tiles by the front door. By all means get it. Much easier to keep clean, and it will significantly increase carpet life. For an even nicer touch, have a recess left in the tiling, dimensioned so as to accept a standard doormat for brushing dirt of your shoes before you step on the carpet.

Fig. 9.8. Six-panel interior doors are better than flat-panel hollow-core doors.

Fig. 9.9. French patio doors seal much better than standard sliding doors.

All Rooms

1. No heating registers or air returns in traffic areas (if there are, get the factory to relocate them; they can even be placed in the walls). Also make sure there isn't one near the island in the kitchen. Check where you are going to put your bed. You don't want a heat vent right under it. What about the living areas? Are there any vents right in the middle of the rooms? Such minor details can make a huge difference in how liveable your home is.

2. 30-inch minimum interior doors wherever possible.

3. Metal mini blinds (not plastic).

Additional Recommended Options

Here is a list of additional options to seriously consider if they are within your budget:

Figs. 9.10. (left) and 9.11 (right). Roof pitch compared. The single-wide on the left has the standard 3:12 pitch, while the double-wide on the right has a more residential-looking 4:12 pitch at a minor cost extra—if specified at the time the home is first ordered.

Exterior

1. 4:12 pitch roof (meaning 4 inches of rise per horizontal foot). Most manufactured homes come with a nominal 3:12 pitch, and the problems you can run into with such a slight pitch are threefold: Number one, the rainwater and melting snow won't run off the roof at a substantial speed, so when the water gets to the edge, it goes around the edge of the shingles then back up the backside. This reduces the life of your roof. Number two, the roof decking will get wet from the water going under the shingles. Finally, the steeper pitch makes your manufactured home look more like a house.

2. Vinyl siding, which will last a lifetime without need for painting. Hardboard siding is better than it used to be, but it's still not that great and needs frequent painting. Besides, manufacturers tend to hide flaws caused by the nails with putty, which can make your house look like a "connect the dots game." And as for metal siding, well, it's got "trailer home" written all over it... Make sure any vinyl siding is installed over Tyvek or similar wind barrier and attached to 8-inch backer boards that have first been attached to the exterior walls of the house.

Fig. 9.12. Dormers over the home's entry and living area add interest to the roof line and a more spacious feeling inside the home.

3. Fiber-cement lap siding as a (more attractive and ecologically sounder) alternative to vinyl. It has a 50-year warranty. Make sure you are satisfied with how the manufacturer applies this product to the house. It is even available in colors that never need painting (assuming you don't want a different color).

4. Recessed entry. You want to get out of the rain, right? It's also more residential looking.

5. 30-lb. minimum roof load. In most parts of the country, that will be adequate. If you live where it snows a lot, you'll need an 80-lb. roof load.

6. French doors instead of sliding patio doors. They seal better and don't have the inherent problems of sliding glass doors.

7. Built-on dormer. This is a peak, or gable, that is built on the roof. It breaks up the flat roof line and adds interesting angles to your home. Make sure it is placed so no valley, or channel, is created over the front door. A raging waterfall over your head may be fun for summer vacations only.

8. Aluminum-covered eaves and fascia.

9. Foundation-ready chassis. This option is necessary if the home will be placed on a solid poured perimeter foundation or a basement.

Fig. 9.13. Take a look under sinks and washbasins, as well as behind the toilets. Make sure there are shut-off valves in both the hot and cold water lines. These are plastic, but they should really be copper tubing with brass valves.

Steven Taylor photo

All Rooms

1. Painted, solid wood door molding. Commonly used is a particle board product wrapped with a simulated-woodgrain vinyl material. The vinyl can pull away from the molding, and if there is a smoker in the house, it can discolor.

2. Rounded corners. This softens the look and feel of your home.

3. 4- or 6-panel doors. They are heavier than standard hollow-core doors, insulate sound better, and have better hinges.

4. Baseboard moldings. These are more residential looking and protect the walls when you vacuum.

5. Interior walls insulated for sound and heat.

6. Lever-style door handles.

7. Tape and texture, at least in the living areas.

Kitchen

1. Stove upgraded one step. You'll enjoy the timer and clock. You may want to take the credit for this appliance and buy your own, and add the price of what you want to install to the price of the house.

2. A larger refrigerator than the standard (18 cu. ft. minimum). Gives you more room, and it can accommodate an ice maker.

3. A built-in microwave or microwave-hood combination This will save some badly needed counter space.

4. A deep stainless steel sink. Porcelain sinks can crack if you drop a skillet on them. Make sure it is at least 8 inches deep—any less, and it will hardly hold a plate and a cup.

5. An extra bank of drawers. One bank of four or five drawers is not enough. Order at least one more for storage.

Utility Room

1. A gas furnace and gas water heater. They are generally better prod-
    ucts than their electric counterparts. If you have access to gas, get
    them. Gas water heaters have quicker recovery and are cheaper to
    operate. Even more economic are tankless (or "flow- through")
    water heaters, but they can make you wait for hot water a bit
    longer. The clothes dryer should also be gas rather than electric.

2. Large fiber glass or vitreous china utility sink—not plastic—with
    tiled backsplash.

Master Bath

1. Two washbasins with a mirror and light sconces on either side of
    the mirrors. Even if you don't need them, they will help with resale.

2. Separate stall shower (make sure it's one-piece fiberglass or better).

3. Medicine cabinet.

4. Bank of drawers.

Other Bathrooms

1. Medicine cabinet.

2. Bank of drawers.

Master Bedroom

1. Cathedral ceiling or recessed ceiling.

2. Walk-in closet.

Non-Factory Options

Here's a list of options you may want to purchase yourself, instead of
from the home's manufacturer, allowing you to obtain items of a better
quality and/or appearance:

Kitchen

1   Appliances.

Electrical

1.   Ceiling fan.

2.   A programmable thermostat, such as a Honeywell. Many manufactured homes come with a cheap plastic thermostat.

Master Bath

1.   Towel bar, soap dish, and tissue holders.

Other Bathrooms

1.   Towel bar, soap dish, and tissue holder.

Living Room

1.   Wood-burning or pellet stove.

2.   Valances.

Unnecessary Factory Options

Here is a list of options the manufacturer may offer but which you should avoid.

1.   Skylights. The plastic ones tend to turn cloudy. The glass ones are better but, like the plastic ones, can eventually leak.

2.   Swamp cooler. Please don't cut a hole in your roof. In time it will leak. Besides, a swamp cooler on your roof makes your home look like a trailer.

3.   Ceiling fans. Buy them at a hardware store or home- improvement center for less and get a better choice of styles.

4. Telephone, cable TV, and Internet cable jacks. Decide exactly where you need them and have them installed by an independent contractor (or learn to do it yourself—it's not rocket science). If the factory installs them, they may finish up in the wrong places.

5. Storm doors. Manufacturers offer cheap doors. Don't buy them, because you can buy better ones yourself for less.

6. Towel bar and toilet paper holders. Buy them for less and get nicer ones at a hardware store.

7. Outswing doors. Avoid them. You will lose heat and energy, and they tell the world, "hey, this is really just a trailer home."

8. Metal roof or siding. Don't. It's no fun sealing your roof or waxing the siding every fall, nor is it particularly attractive to put a bunch of old car tires on the roof to prevent the metal from flapping in the wind

9. Wood-burning stoves, pellet stoves, fireplaces. We recommend you purchase none of these from the home's manufacturer. Their selection in wood-burning or pellet stoves is limited and the hearth will

Fig. 9.14. A nice elevated deck with wide steps, sturdy railings, and a walkway.

be mediocre at best. Forget the fireplace completely: it'll be cheap and cheesy, not to mention its inefficiency. Wood-burning stoves and pellet stoves are an attractive way to heat your house while providing a cozy atmosphere. Hire an independent specialist to install your choice of stove and vent it out through a wall. Avoid cutting holes in the roof.

10. Log siding, cedar siding. It's a nice idea, but do you really want to treat your siding every year? Besides, the rust stains running down your house from the nails used to apply the siding just don't look good.

11. Dining room chandelier. Just specify the home be wired for a ceiling light, then get your own at a hardware store or home improvement center. It will be cheaper and you'll have a wider selection to choose from.

Optioning Methods

Let us summarize the different ways to option your home:

1. Take the credit on the option, get a cost on its replacement, and add it to the price of the home.

2. Take the option that's standard in the home and then change it later yourself.

Now that you have an idea as to how we recommend you option your home, let us tell you why. In the early- to mid-1990s, the cost of lumber and options to put in your home was reasonable. Then, many dealers were hit with lumber surcharges and option cost increases. The same home cost perhaps 50% more in 2020 than it did in 1994.

What we see many dealers doing to cut their cost and reduce the selling price of a home, is show their display homes with flash—the home on display may have vinyl siding and a 4:12 pitch roof to catch your eye—but inside, the home is "stripped." It may have plastic sinks, fixtures, and hardware, and while it may still have vinyl-clad energy-efficient windows, it may have only 2 x 4 exterior walls with minimal insulation, perhaps with a R-11 rating.

It is important to have 2 x 6 exterior walls with R-21 insulation. The dealer may have cut down on the ceiling insulation too.

There are many more examples of this, but you get the idea. It is best to order your home with the options you want. Don't fall for a sell job on a dealer stock home unless you have seen the option sheet and it has everything you want in the way of options and upgrades.

Other Details

We need to drive this point home, so we are going to say this as plainly as we can: Do not take the standard carpet or be talked into buying the manufacturer's so-called "upgrade" carpet. None of it will last more than a few years. Someday, maybe, this will change, but for now, your best deal will be to go to a carpet store and buy at least 52-ounce carpet. The carpet pad needs to be at least a 6-pound pad—the thickness does not necessarily matter as much as the weight. If your pocket book allows for it, go for a 7-pound pad, which is even better.

Salespeople do not understand most of this process, so you have to understand it well enough yourself to be able to specify it. Many times a factory spec sheet will show a 30-gallon water heater standard, and then an optional 40-gallon water heater for $95. The 40 gallon water heater does not cost just $95. The $95 is how much more you will be charged for the 40-gallon water heater than for the 30-gallon water heater that is standard in the house.

Kitchen appliances work the same way. The dealer says that the standard stove that comes in your home can be upgraded for $65, right? The stove probably cost the factory $220. The factory in turn makes a profit on the stove by charging the dealer $320. So your total charge is $385. Go to an appliance store instead, where you can probably get the same stove for much less.

Concerning electrical wiring, you want to make sure it is copper and a 4-wire system. This has become standard on new site-built homes, and it ought to be standard in factory-built housing. No more fire traps, please.

Wheelchair Access

Manufactured homes can be handicapped-conducive. Here is what to do. Order the widest interior doors possible to get a wheelchair through. If you need a higher toilet, it will probably have to be installed as a replacement after the house is delivered. However, grab bars for the shower and toilet areas should be installed at the factory to be covered by warranty. You will have to define heights and other dimensions for the assembly line to properly place them.

Formaldehyde

Often you will notice a distinct odor upon entering a new manufactured home. It is caused by formaldehyde, which is used as a bonding agent in many of the building and trim materials used. Some people are very sensitive to it and others aren't. Our experience has been that after a few months, the smell usually dissipates and is unnoticeable. However, some people experience burning eyes and lungs. Well insulated, energy-efficient manufactured homes will hold air in so well that mechanical venting may be required to get rid of the odor. In addition, crack some windows.

IMPORTANT HEALTH NOTICE

Some of the building materials used in this home emit formaldehyde. Eye, nose, and throat irritation, headache, nausea, and a variety of asthma-like symptoms, including shortness of breath, have been reported as a result of formaldehyde exposure. Elderly persons and young children, as well as anyone with a history of asthma, allergies, or lung problems, may be at greater risk. Research is continuing on the possible long-term effects of exposure to formaldehyde.

Reduced ventilation resulting from energy efficiency standards may allow formaldehyde and other contaminants to accumulate in the indoor air. Additional ventilation to dilute the indoor air may be obtained from a passive or mechanical ventilation system offered by the manufacturer. Consult your dealer for information about the ventilation options offered with this home.

High indoor temperatures and humidity raise formaldehyde levels. When a home is to be located in areas subject to extreme summer temperatures, an air-conditioning system can be used to control indoor temperature levels. Check the comfort cooling certificate to determine if this home has been equipped or designed for the installation of an air conditioning system.

If you have any questions regarding the health effects of formaldehyde, consult your doctor or local health department.

Fig. 9.15. A typical formaldehyde warning label. It is a health notice as required by law to be displayed in every home set up for viewing on a dealer's lot.

10

Make it Look Like a Home

I N THIS CHAPTER, we will give you some ideas for "disguising" your manufactured home to look and feel more like a site-built home. Some of these points have already been mentioned elsewhere in the book, but here they are presented in a more comprehensive form. We will also proffer some suggestions for getting the desired features most economically.

Outside Appearance

In this first section, we'll be looking at the exterior of the home, and see what can be done to get its appearance out of the "mental trailer park" into the mainstream, so it looks and "feels" more like the substantial home you can feel proud to own. To better understand the process, let's take a look at some pictures of "standard" manufactured homes, like those depicted in Figs. 10.1 and 10.2 (and some elsewhere in the book).

We will try to analyze what makes it so obvious that these homes, though probably perfectly livable inside, look too much like "trailers" instead of "homes." Here's our list of visually disturbing features:

1. The home next door is also obviously a similar manufactured home, i.e. you can tell immediately that home in question is situated in a manufactured home community.

2. The skirting that hides the wheels and substructure is corrugated sheet metal and clearly says "skirting," rather than looking like it belongs there as an integral part of the home.

3. The buildings are long and skinny, just like early manufactured homes.

4. The home's length is accentuated by the fact that its facade is uninterrupted at the roof line.

5. In other cases, the home seems even longer by having added a garage in line with the building itself (e.g. Fig. 2.1 on page 19).

6. The roofs have shallow 3:12 pitch with only minimal overhang.

7. The siding looks like corrugated metal (a perfectly good material—if only it didn't *look* like corrugated metal).

8. The windows are small, and the shutters (which are not functional but merely decorative anyway) are too small for the windows, making it too obvious they're fake.

9. There is a narrow stairway and a tiny landing leading straight up to the front door, without a front porch or deck.

10. The entrance to the house is very plain with a functional but ugly bare metal front door.

MHI photo

Left and facing page: Figs. 10.1 and 10.2. For a residential look—and feel—avoid making your house look like these.

From this follow some conclusions, and we will give you some simple suggestions for how to avoid those problems.

1. Check out the homes next door to yours before you choose yours, and specify features that make it look different. Perhaps all you need do is a different orientation—like East-West, if the neighbor's homes are oriented North-South.

2. Place the home on a poured concrete or a concrete block perimeter foundation, or even just a brick skirting (if it's permissible in your area—don't try that in earthquake country).

3. Don't be too tempted by the cost advantage of a single-wide over double- and triple-wides. And if you really can't afford the latter, you can save even more by not choosing the biggest single-wide you can get, which doesn't look as skinny as bigger models.

4. Specify a dormer over the front door, which should not be centered, and at least one other area, such as the living room. You can also add a (generous) enclosed or partially enclosed entrance lobby or front porch at the front door.

5. Don't add the garage in line with the building, but put it in an L-configuration, or alternately in a separate building, connected to the home by a short covered walkway.

6. Specify at least a 4:12 pitch roof. That looks much better, and rain-water will drain off much better to boot.

7. Check out all the options for siding, from vinyl to real wood (in which case you should be prepared to repaint the exterior frequently).

8. Specify larger windows, in clusters of 2 or 3, and if you like the look of fake shutters, at least make sure they are wide enough to cover the window if they were real.

9. Interrupt and angle the stairs up to the front door, with a platform between the two portions, and make the entry landing or front porch at least 5 ft. by 5 ft., preferably bigger.

10. Use a residential type front door, with an armored glass window, an attractive door lock-handle, a brass mail slot and a "kick plate," matched coach lanterns or sconces on both sides of the door, a small horizontal window over the door, and long, narrow windows on either side of the door. Big brass house numbers don't hurt either. No fake columns please.

Interior Improvements

Here is a list of things that will make your house look and feel more residential inside. Although this list is by no means exhaustive, it presents the areas where most impact can be obtained most effectively at a modest outlay. See Chapter 14 for some advice on deciding who should do the actual upgrading of individual components.

Paint and Texture

Flat paint is cheap and easy to apply, and that's what you're likely to get, and to keep costs down, it will probably have been applied in too thin a layer and with inadequate (or even without) primer. Fortunately, it will probably be white, and it's sure to be latex paint. That makes it easy to repaint using higher quality paint and a more attractive color scheme. Get advice on suitable color combinations from any paint supplier (either from their web site or from their in-store consultant).

The most important thing to note is that flat paint is a bad choice for the trim, as well as for kitchen and baths. You need semi-gloss, which not only looks more attractive, but also is more scuff-resistant and easier to keep clean. Yes, you can repaint those areas yourself, but before you do, try to realize that it's not true that any idiot can paint. You need some instructions if you want it to look good. Again, the paint companies will provide all the schooling you need in the form of easy-to-read pamphlets or on their web site. Don't skip those!

Don't skimp on paint brushes. Buy just one or two big (2½ or 3 inch) high-quality brushes, like those made by Purdy; they will set you back some $30 each, but they're worth every penny. Rinse them out thoroughly immediately after use, and let them dry with a piece of newspaper carefully wrapped around the bristles to preserve their shape.

Here's a little trick for getting the smooth look that you thought could only be achieved with a spray gun: Mix a teaspoon full of dishwashing liquid (*not* dishwasher detergent, please) in with your gallon can of paint, or 5 drops if you use a quart can. Stir in well, but don't shake the can, so the paint doesn't get bubbles in it. The original paint (whether primer or flat latex) must first be sanded perfectly smooth, otherwise its blemishes will always show through, even with the smooth new paint. And did you know brush painting puts on considerably more paint (which translates into better protection) than spray paint?

Flooring

In the bedrooms, choose high-quality carpet with a heavy-duty pad, and coordinate the color of the carpet with the paint color scheme. (That doesn't mean all should be the same color, but shades and tints should be selected within the same color range; paint companies have pamphlets that are very helpful if you don't have a feel for it yourself.)

In the living room, go either for high-quality carpet or real hardwood flooring. It's OK to use "engineered" hardwood, which is easy to install, but don't use laminate (such as Pergo), because it looks great only in a printed color brochure, but horribly fake in real life—it even sounds fake when you walk on it.

In the bathrooms, kitchen, and utility room, consider ceramic tiles instead of sheet vinyl. It's incredibly durable, looks luxurious, and is easy to install with the help of one of the many good home-project books out there. We've bought tile at home-improvement centers for as little as 79¢ per square foot, but even if you "splurge" and pay twice as much for nice tile, it's still a bargain, and a handsome bargain at that.

Entrance and Living & Dining Room

Whether just areas of the same space or separate rooms, these should all give a feeling of space. That's why we like to have raised ceilings (achieved with dormers) in at least one of those areas. The windows should be large, preferably tall, even if not necessarily very wide. Drapes should be floor-to-ceiling, and generously pleated.

A cheap and easy way to achieve more apparent ceiling height is by using what's referred to as "cathedral ceiling." It's a somewhat pompous term for what amounts to little more than leaving the ceiling out altogether. To achieve this effect, the roof trusses are reinforced and spaced more widely than in the rest of the house, and the inside of the roof slope is insulated and covered either with wood paneling or drywall.

Kitchen

Upgrade the kitchen cabinets with solid wood doors and find some attractive handles and drawer pulls. We've found very attractive modern looking pulls and handles at a home improvement center for less than $1 a piece. Shop around.

Yes, you can have granite counter tops in your manufactured home! We found beautiful 25 inch by 8 ft. granite counter tops for as little as $89 (really, that's not a typo). You can also spend 10 times as

M-H photo

Fig. 10.3. The inside matters too. This kitchen says "mobile home." Why? For one, there's a 3:12 sloping ceiling, emphasized by the dark wall-to-ceiling trim. Of course, those plastic mini blinds in front of low windows and that bare ceiling light fixture don't help either. And if you'd see it in color, you'd notice the bright blue fake marble counter tops.

much, but you'd be hard put to tell the difference. Of course, cutouts for the sink, etc. do cost extra, but it still all ads up to a reasonable price for the perceived value. There is no need to also use granite for the backsplashes, because tiling the entire area between the counter top and the upper cabinets is more effective and looks great too (remember those cheap tiles we mentioned?).

Color coordinate the appliances as much as possible. If the range is white, make sure the dishwasher, the fridge, the range hood, and the microwave, and even minor things like the toaster and the coffee maker, are also white. Taking the color coordination a step further, you can choose the same color for some other features in your kitchen, like the lights, the drawer pulls, or even the pots and pans.

Bathrooms

Here too, color coordination is a cheap and easy way to achieve an attractive appearance. Tiling the shower or tub enclosures and the area above the wash basin, and indeed the entire walls (as well as the floors) also helps give your bathroom an air of luxury and quality.

High-quality faucets can be absurdly expensive, but with luck you'll probably find attractively coordinated faucets. The same goes for towel rails and other minor fixtures. You need sconce lighting on either side of the mirrors as well as an overhead light/fan. We've found $15 sconces that look and perform like designer lights. Shop around.

Electrical

Decor switches look very much more attractive and modern than conventional toggle switches (which are quite a bit cheaper and just as functional, so don't bother in less visible areas like utility rooms).

Don't settle for the default light fixtures that come standard with the home. But don't run out to an expensive lighting store either. Home improvement centers have all sorts of attractive lights at reasonable prices, and it doesn't take much to install them yourself. Just don't forget to turn the power off by triggering the circuit breaker before you touch any electrical wiring. And hire a handyman if you're not sure of your abilities in this field. There's usually no need to hire an (expensive) electrician for this kind of work: it's not rocket science.

The Energy-Efficient Home

I N RECENT YEARS, the concept "Energy Star Compliant" has become a familiar term: it's a measure of the home's overall energy efficiency. In the Pacific Northwest, this concept follows on the heels of what used to be known as "Super Good Cents" program. The higher energy efficiency is primarily achieved with better insulation. Especially in areas such as the Southwest, where air conditioners are more common than in the Pacific North-West, it is equally important to have a well-insulated home with dual-pane windows.

The goal of the Energy Star Program, which was originally intended for site-built housing, is to motivate builders to increase energy efficiency and life-cycle cost savings through an integrated design and certification process. To qualify for the Energy Star label, a home must use at least 30% less energy for heating, cooling and water heating than the CABO Model Energy Code requires for the home. Manufactured home builders have achieved this by not only increasing R-values for insulation, but also by tightening ducts and using more efficient HVAC systems and water heaters, as well as heat-reflective roof designs.

There is an interesting (and somewhat ironic) history behind the granddaddy of the Energy Star rating: Around 1990, Bonneville Power, in the Pacific Northwest wanted to sell more electric power. So they got together with manufactured home companies and agreed on a deal in which, if the factories would produce an energy-efficient home with an electric furnace, Bonneville Power would send a $3,500 rebate to the home buyer, thus encouraging the use of electric power, but also puting some money back into the home buyer's pocket—and encouraging more energy-efficient electric homes.

The manufactured home companies thus began to produce more energy-efficient manufactured homes. These had 2 x 6 exterior walls, 2 x 6 floor joists, and engineered roof trusses. They also had dual-pane, vinyl-clad windows. In addition, manufacturers began to increase the R-values (which is a measurement of insulation and its effectiveness— the higher the number, the better).

This program became extremely successful, and the sale of manu- factured homes in that part of the country increased dramatically. De- mand increased each year, costing Bonneville Power millions of dollars, which motivated them to reduce the rebate to $2,500. Also, the rebate was taken out of the home buyer's hands and sent to the manu- facturer. Still, orders increased and the popularity of manufactured homes kept growing. Later, the $2,500 rebate was reduced to $1,500, and finally completely dropped in 1995.

Depending on where you live, there may be a similar program in place now to encourage energy efficiency. The Energy Star program is administered by the Energy Star Homes Program of the U.S. Environ- mental Protection Agency, with the website *http://www.epa.gov/homes*. In addition, several states have their own office to administer the pro- gram.

Energy-Star Compliant homes are extremely energy-efficient, and we strongly recommend them as something well worth spending some extra bucks for. It will enhance not only the current *and* resale value of the home, but also the home's comfort.

In connection with energy-efficiency programs, some misconcep- tions were spawned that we would like to correct to help you make an informed buying decision. Most of these rules apply to today's Energy Star Compliant home programs. Here are some of the currently appli- cable facts:

1. The home does not necessarily have to have the thicker 2 x 6 exte- rior walls, as long as the overall energy efficiency is attained.

2. The home does not have to be either all gas or all electric, as long as the required energy efficiency is maintained.

3. The minimum R-value figures for a well-insulated home are R-22 for the floor, R-33 for the ceiling, and R-19 for the walls.

4. To achieve the required energy efficiency, the home may have only a limited amount of glazing (window area) depending on interior floor space.

5. There's no need for argon gas between the panes of glass in the windows, as long as they are vinyl-clad and double glazed. If the dealer offers vinyl-clad windows as an option, don't go for it, because vinyl-clad windows should be standard in all homes anyway. No need to pay extra! Finally, low-E glass. This has a film between the two panes of glass. It will act as an ultraviolet radiation buffer, which will result in fewer fade marks on your furniture and your carpet. Here is the difference:
   - ❏ Clear glass windows have a U-value of .45.
   - ❏ Low-E windows have a U-value of .37.

The lower the U-value, the better the insulation.

You may or may not be versed in building codes and what they mean, but you should know the meaning of the R- and U-values. The U-value is a number that expresses the house's overall energy rating. The smaller the number the better.

The R-value is a measure of the insulation quality of a particular insulating material, and it's primarily a function of its thickness. The higher the number, the better the insulation quality. Common numbers for Energy Star Compliant homes are as follows:
- ❏ R-33 ceiling insulation
- ❏ R-49 for ceiling insulation in flat-ceiling triple-wides
- ❏ R-19 wall insulation
- ❏ R-22 floor insulation
- ❏ .37 NFRC-rated dual pane vinyl clad windows with low-E glass.
- ❏ Gaskets around electric wall outlets and other wall penetrations.
- ❏ A specified minimum R-rating for the heat crossover duct and tightened ducting connections.
- ❏ Passive ventilation that provides fresh air even when the HVAC unit is not running.

12
How to Be Your Own Contractor

I N THIS CHAPTER, we will show you how to be your own general contractor and save a bunch of money. This is another step in being in
control of your home-buying process. It's not as hard as you may think.
Dealers love to keep a tight rein on this process because many like to
kick a little extra profit into the costs of your improvements. It doesn't
matter if you're doing a land-home project or putting a single-wide in a
manufactured home community. Overseeing this process will prevent
heartache and an empty wallet.

Be prepared for certain new challenges to arise and a great many
details to cover, but you will find contractors and building inspectors
that are willing to work with you if you follow a logical process. The
following pages will give you a step-by-step procedure to follow.

There will be deviations from time to time, but this is normal. Each
project is different, but if you follow this systematic procedure, you'll
be prepared for those too.

Placing a Home in a Manufactured Home Community

Follow to the simple steps outlined below if you are putting a home in a
community. You may have to fall out of sequence from time to time, but
this gives you the starting points. It will be worthwhile—remember,
many dealers who tell you they arrange your improvements mark

them up with or without a contractor's knowledge to make more profit for themselves.

1. Secure financing. Reread Chapter 5, dealing with financing, if necessary. This may be a situation where you have no other option than to finance at the dealership—but try a mortgage company first.

2. Go and inspect manufactured home community, get their monthly rent and a list of covenants and select the one that suits you best.

3. Select the home that best suits your needs.

4. Get the dimensions of the home.

5. Go back home and call a skirting company and get a bid. Make sure it is vinyl-clad skirting with a lifetime warranty and that it has venting. We would advise against skirting that is made to look like "river rock," because it is and looks fake, and it can warp and buckle due to temperature changes.

6. Get bids on the improvements you would like—decks, garage, awnings, gutters, air-conditioning. Get at least two bids on each item.

7. Get the bids in writing and take them to the bank or dealership, depending on where you are financing.

8. The contract to purchase should have these improvements written on it with the cost next to them. Make sure the home price is written separately from the improvement costs.

9. Write it up—after negotiation of course.

10. If you are taking delivery of a home from the dealer's stock, agree upon a move-in date you can live with and put it in the contract.

11. If you are ordering a home from the factory, agree upon a move-in date and put it in the contract.

12. Keep the original bids for improvements.

13. Make sure improvements are done to your satisfaction.

14. Once the house arrives and is set up, go through it with the option sheet and make sure everything you paid for is there. If it is not, make the dealer correct the situation. The option sheet is considered a part of the contract to purchase.

Placing a Home on Your Own Land

If you are starting with bare land with no improvements, or if you are able to hook up to the city sewer and water, you will have a bigger undertaking. Take a breath. It can be fun.

1. Secure financing. Reread Chapter 5, on financing, if necessary. Don't finance at a dealership.

2. Go and shop for the home that best meets your needs and budget. See Chapter 7, on price and negotiation. Write it up.

3. Get the dimensions of the house.

4. Look at land with a realtor.

5. Call the contractors. Get at least two bids per improvement. Here are some possible improvements you may need for bare land:

   ❑ Foundation

   ❑ Well

   ❑ Septic tank

   ❑ Power

   ❑ Gas

   ❑ Driveway

   ❑ Garage

6. If you are within reach of city sewer and water, get bids to hook up from the city.

7. Apply for a building permit at the building department, taking along a copy of the purchase contract for your home.

8. Once you have a permit, have the contractor do a perc test. This can take several days, so start early.

9. If you are ordering your home, find out the time frame of delivery.

10. If you need a road up to your lot, have it built first.

11. Have the foundation built.

12. Have the well dug and the septic tank put in place.

13. Have the garage built.

14. Make sure a representative from the dealership comes to plan the best way to bring the house onto your site.

15. Have the home delivered, installed on your foundation, and prepared for your move-in.

16. A final inspection will be done by an appraiser and sent to the bank for final review. This inspection report is referred to as a "442."

17. The bank will draw up closing documents and send them to a title company.

18. The title company will call you and set up a time for you to close your loan.

19. Once the closing is done, the title company will disperse funds to the dealer, contractors, and any other parties involved.

A Note on Deposits

When it comes time to sign a purchase agreement, the salesman will ask you for a certain amount of down payment. Many times, the dealer will tell you they need 5 or 10 % of the purchase price of the home to order it from the factory. Dealers like to blame this on the factory. You may hear, "The factory has to have this money to begin production of your home."

This isn't true. It's just one way of getting money out of you. Wouldn't you prefer to hold on to your money, earning interest, as long as possible?

Here's what you do: Since you've already been approved at a bank or by a mortgage company, you know what your down payment will be, and that is what you bring to closing at the title company. Do not give it to the dealership. Give them $100 or $200, tops. Tell them you will have your bank send them a commitment letter. The dealership will get all their money at closing. Don't let them buffalo you. If they refuse to order the home without a huge amount of money up front, tell them it's your way or no way. They may frown and squirm, but they need your business. If they still give you a hard time, take your business elsewhere. This industry has become so competitive, you *will* find a dealer who'll do it your way

Let us give you a scenario of what happened when a home buyer gave the dealer too much money. Everything seemed to be in place. Mr. Buyer had an accepted offer on the land. He had bids on improvements. He had a home picked out—and unfortunately let the nice salesman talk him into giving the dealership $20,000 up front. Then he went and got financing at a bank. The home was perfect, and Mrs. Buyer was happy too. The problem arose when they wanted to start improvements on the land.

The land seller wanted to be paid in full before anyone ever touched the property. The banker had not been aware of this and did not structure the loan to be staged (meaning there would first be a closing on the land, and later another one on the house and other improvements). The cost of the land was $15,000, and all Mr. Buyer's money was where? At the dealership. Mr. Buyer asked the dealer to give some of the money back so he could pay off the land seller. Of course the dealer said, "No." What a surprise...

So Mr. Buyer had to grovel to the land seller to take $10,000 (which he got from his IRA) and a note for $5,000 payable in 60 days. This process took an additional 30 days. No help from the dealer and no help from the bank. You see the importance of the sequence of steps that we outlined for you?

13
Materials and Construction

IT IS IMPORTANT to be aware of the types of materials used in your house and how those materials work together in the finished product. In this chapter, we have put together a smattering of areas for you to think about. Remember that we are neither engineers nor contractors. Our point of view is from experience and from talking to set-up crews in the field. Also remember that the way manufactured homes are built differs from the way site-built homes are. Because of the code that manufactured homes are built to, some of the building materials can be of lower quality. You must be the final judge. Let's start at the top and work down.

Roof

Most manufactured homes come standard with a shallow-pitch roof, such as "3:12," meaning there is a 3 inch rise for every 12 inches of roof width. A steeper pitch, even if it's only 4:12 looks better and sheds rainwater better.

The Uniform Building Code for site-built homes says that there must be "felt" (felt paper—a moisture barrier) applied to the roof decking before the shingles are attached. Recently, modern materials have begun to be used for this same purpose. Not all manufactured home manufacturers use it, but it is highly recommended.

The trusses that support the roof of a site-built home are generally 2 x 6 or the increasingly popular "I-joists." On manufactured homes they are usually 2 x 2 or smaller for a 3:12 pitch roof. For a 4:12 roof, they should be 2 x 3 or preferably 2 x 4. Get written confirmation of the size that will be used.

Exterior Walls

Siding is also something to consider. For durability and low maintenance, our choice would be vinyl siding or something similar that requires no painting. If you choose hardboard, be prepared to paint it frequently, and possibly replace it every ten years or so. We suggest you repaint it with high-quality exterior paint immediately after delivery of the home, since the factory paint is almost always inadequate.

Hardboard siding is a wood-based material that is made by binding wood fibers together under pressure. If the siding should become damaged, repairs need to be made quickly, because exposed to the weather, the material would soon start to disintegrate. For the same reason, it should be kept thoroughly primed and painted. Some type of sealer that matches the paint should be used. If you don't make repairs, water will infiltrate the siding, causing it to swell. Don't use nails or screws to attach anything to your hardboard siding, because they create holes through which moisture could penetrate, causing serious damage.

Hardboard and wood siding materials come in different types and qualities. Some manufacturers use wood cedar shingles, which we do not recommend. They change color from red to grey and you will have to stain them every year or so if you want them to look fresh and new. On the other hand, if you plan to install the home in a rustic area for recreation, the natural cedar siding will fit in very nicely.

Caulking is used a lot with hardboard siding. This is done to keep moisture from getting behind trim around windows, etc. Caulking can become brittle and it can absorb dirt and oil from the air. You will have to inspect the caulking every year, and you usually have to replace some of it, preferably using the more expensive, but much longer-lasting polyurethane caulk.

Take into account the fact that many manufacturers do not use a wind barrier before the siding is applied. Tyvek or some other brand is used on site-built houses, and we strongly urge you to make sure it is specified on your manufactured home too.

The siding must not be nailed straight to the studs from which the walls are constructed. There must be rigid wall panels, such as ⅝ in. thick plywood or oriented-strand board nailed to the studs to make the wall into a rigid structure. Tyvek is then stapled to this material to provide a wind barrier, and the siding goes on top of that. The siding panels are installed with enough overlap to cover any nail or screw holes used to attach the individual panels. In the case of vinyl siding, the panels are attached to 8-inch backer boards.

Sometimes the siding is not installed until the home reaches the site, which is a nice way to avoid showing the marriage lines in double- and triple-wides.

Interior Walls

Moving inside, site-built homes use ⅜ to ½ inch drywall. We have yet to see a manufactured home with more than ½ inch. If your budget allows, stay away from that thin ⅜-inch drywall wrapped with wallpaper. It is very thin, and if a hole or blemish occurs on one of the walls, you'd have to replace the entire panel. Besides, by then the particular wallpaper has probably been discontinued by the manufacturer, leaving you in a bind with no way to match the pattern.

Next, compare how the drywall is attached to the wall studs. Site-built homes will use drywall screws, and many manufactured homes do, too. However, some use foam with a chemical reaction to bond the drywall to the studs. Our experience with homes using this

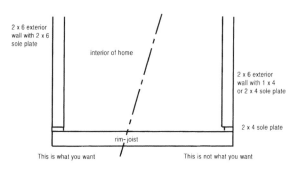

Fig. 11.1. Comparing a 2 x 6 sole plate used with 2 x 6 walls (left) with a narrower 1 x 4 or 2 x 4 sole plate (right). Although the narrower sole plate is not a code violation in most states, it is not satisfactory.

process has not been very good. The foam tends to squeeze between the studs and the drywall, making a bulge appear along the stud line. Maybe someday the technique will be perfected, but for now it makes for uneven walls and ceilings.

Preferably, the home should have taped and textured corners, wherever the joints where the walls meet the ceiling and where wall meets wall. A cheaper, and uglier, way found on many low-end homes is a thin bead of caulking running down this very visible joint. The caulk will dry and become brittle and can pull away. This won't look good, and you'll have to re-caulk it again and again.

Floor and Substructure

Most site-built homes have plywood or OSB (oriented strand board) floor decking that's anything from ¾ to ⅞ inch thick. In manufactured housing, most manufacturers use the old "mobile home decking," which is a product made of particle board that's impregnated with resin to make it water resistant. The width of the decking is usually 4 feet, and the length is whatever the width of the section of the home happens to be—12, 14, or 16 feet. Nails are used to attach the decking to the floor joists, and occasionally glue is added.

We would recommend looking for either 4 x 8 ft. sheets of plywood or OSB decking. The 4 x 8 sheets are applied to the floor system in an offset pattern, which avoids the problem of "crowning." Crowning occurs when a long piece of decking is used, say 4 x 14 ft. The weight of the exterior walls is supported by the perimeter of the floor system and can cause the center of the floor to bulge up.

There are different sizes of floor joists available, 2 x 4, 2 x 6, and 2 x 8 inches. 2 x 6 works fine; however, 2 x 8 is twice as strong, whereas 2 x 4 is only half as strong, so we advise against 2 x 4 floor joists.

A lot of manufacturers use a skinny 1 x 4 sole plate (the bottom framing member of the exterior walls). You should make sure you get one that is 2 x 6 instead; otherwise you can't attach baseboard in the home.

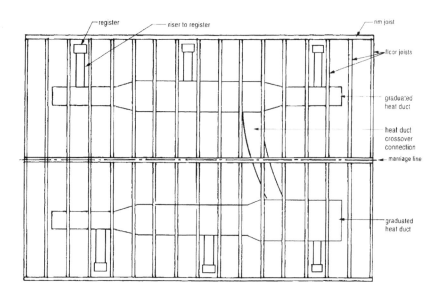

Above: Fig. 11.2. Heating system with graduated ducts, resulting in even heat distribution. The registers are along the outside walls, away from the traffic pattern.

Below: Fig. 11.3. Conventional "one-size-fits-all" heating ducts, resulting in poor heat distribution and registers poorly placed in the traffic areas.

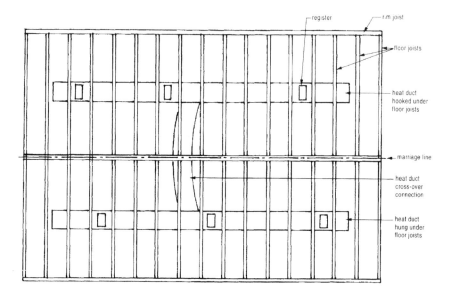

The Heating System

Another major difference between manufactured and site-built homes is the heating system. First, the furnace itself will be different. In the Northwest, the two big suppliers to factories are Coleman and Intertherm. Their products are OK, but definitely not top-of-the-line. The efficiency of gas and electric furnaces is about 80%. You can get their ratings in BTU (British Thermal Units) for gas and kW (Kilowatts) for electric units.

Many manufacturers put the same size furnace in all their models, regardless of the size of the house. It seems to make sense that a 2,500 sq. ft. triple-wide would require a larger furnace than a 900 sq. ft. single-wide. For larger double- and triple-section homes, we recommend ordering a furnace that is larger than the manufacturer's standard furnace. Make sure the right model is installed initially.

Most manufactured homes also give you a one-size-fits-all heating duct system built into the floor of your home. This means that the duct is the same dimension the entire length of your house. Our experience with living in a factory-built house with this system is that your utility room, where the furnace is, will be very warm, while the master bathroom, at the other end of the home, will never heat up. Here's the reason: As the air comes out of the bottom of the furnace into the head duct, it loses speed as it travels to the other end of the house. It loses speed because the heat duct does not narrow to keep the same volume of air blowing into each room. Thus, the far end of the home will be cold. To allow the same air speeds, you need a graduated heat duct system, which maintains the same volume of air flowing into every room.

In areas where air conditioning is not required, there are better ways of heating your manufactured home: underfloor radiant heating and "hydrophonic" heating systems, both of which are not only far more comfortable, but also more economical. The former generally use electric coils under the floor, while the latter uses hot water.

Condensation and Ventilation

You may have noticed that manufactured homes have large gaps under the interior doors. It looks awful and you can hear sounds from the other room, but there is a good reason for this: Due to the type of heating and cooling system used in most factory-built homes, the house itself must be used as an air return. The air comes out of the floor register, into a particular room, under the door, and eventually back to where the furnace is located. For more information on this type of design, check out *http://www.HomeEnergy.org* on the web.

Condensation is a problem all manufacturers are concerned about. It may seem odd, but the more energy-efficient and tightly constructed a home is, the more condensation problems it can have. Condensation is the process of vapor (all air contains vaporized water) changing from the gaseous to the liquid state. Warm air absorbs evaporated water much like a sponge. As this warm air gets into contact with colder surfaces, such as exterior windows, walls, and water pipes, it can hold less moisture. Cooling warm air is like squeezing a wet sponge: the moisture comes out, and it collects on your windows and on many other surfaces in your home.

Examples of activities that cause additional water vapor are drying clothes, cooking, bathing, dishwashing, and using gas appliances. However, the biggest contributor of water vapor in your home will be you yourself, by inhalation and perspiration.

Make sure to read your homeowner's manual about how to control condensation. Methods used to control the problem can include exhaust fans, avoiding or reducing use of humidifiers, and cracking windows.

Manufacturers can reduce the problems by using one of two methods: mechanical and passive venting.

❏ Passive venting uses strategically placed vents under the eaves, on the ends of the house, and on the roof.

❏ Mechanical venting exchanges air in the home with the outside air by pressurizing the attic cavity to keep the air circulating.

If you see a manufactured home with little or no venting under the eaves, there is a good chance the home is mechanically vented by a fan somewhere in the attic cavity. The fan is designed to run day and night, 365 days a year. It uses energy, and it tends to get noisier over time.

The advantage of passive venting is that you don't have to worry about mechanical breakdown. It is also silent and energy-efficient.

If your home is set on a foundation, or is skirted for that matter, there are always vents installed under the house to allow air to circulate freely underneath, allowing it to "breathe." A mechanical device is not required in this area.

Survey

In its February 1998 issue, *Consumer Reports* published a survey on consumer satisfaction with, and complaints about, manufactured housing. Below is a summary of the information presented in this survey. What it tells us is that most of the major items of concern with manufactured homes agree with what is pointed out in this book. After surveying 1,029 consumers nationally, its findings include:

1. Manufactured homes can last as long as site-built ones. As with many other things, the more expensive the house, the fewer problems you are likely to have.

2. Eighty-two percent of the respondents were largely satisfied with their manufactured home. A majority had at least one major problem.

3. Owners of homes placed in manufactured home communities felt vulnerable to landlords who had the power to increase space rent.

4. HUD has been a major factor in raising standards of quality in manufactured housing.

The major weak spots the respondents identified were floors, central heating and cooling, plumbing, roofing, windows, doors, and installation. Let's look at each one.

Floors	One fourth of those surveyed had problems with particle board flooring. It can swell and break down if it gets wet.
Central heating and air conditioning	Improper placement of registers resulted in uneven heating and cooling. One fifth of the respondents reported having problems.

Plumbing

Polybutylene pipes may leak. Manufacturers are dropping this product and other cheap plastic piping, but check anyway. Thirty-six percent had problems with plumbing.

Roof

Thirty-one percent of those surveyed had problems with their metal roofs leaking at the seams. Although not so common here in the Northwest, many manufactured homes with metal roofs are still sold in other regions.

Windows and doors

Gaps around doors and windows (broken seals) may be the result of transporting the home from factory to site. Windows of lower quality have their corners joined with fasteners, not a continuous weld. They leak. Thirty-two percent of purchasers had to deal with leaking windows.

Installation

Homes not set on a poured concrete foundation are more susceptible to cracking of tape and texture and "sticking" doors and windows.

Consumer Reports did an excellent job, and even though the survey was done many years ago, most of its conclusions are as valid today as they were at the time they were first written. We highly recommend you read the entire article at a library. (Unfortunately, it is not currently available on the Consumer Reports website.)

14
Customizing Your Home

AS SHOWN on the dealer's lot, the home of your choice will probably still have some features you'd like done differently. We've mentioned the quality (or lack of quality) of the carpeting installed before. However, there are a whole slew of other smaller or bigger details to consider as well. The brand, type, or quality of light fixtures, doorknobs, shutters, bathroom and kitchen fixtures are just a few things that can make the difference between a run-of-the-mill manufactured home and one that bears your personal signature.

Of course, you'll be paying extra to upgrade. In fact, if you're not careful, you may even be charged money to substitute items that don't cost any more than those in the manufacturer's standard package. This chapter will show you how you can minimize the extra costs while getting exactly what you want in your home.

Who'll Do the Work?

There are three basic options for doing the upgrade work, as listed below:

1. Specify the upgrades you want and have the factory do the work for you. Assuming everything is done correctly and you're not

charged excessively for it, this is the easiest way for many upgrades.

2. Have the home shipped "as is" and change out the items at your own expense, either by an outside contractor or by doing the work yourself.

3. Have the item(s) left out of the specification for the home you're ordering and have the brands and models of your choice installed at your own expense, again either by an outside contractor or by doing the work yourself.

For most of the major items, it behooves you to choose option 3, using the technique we outlined on the basis of the carpet example in Chapter 4. You tell the dealer to leave out the standard option and take his (meager) discount and demand an accurate accounting of the number of specific items left out of the package. Then you buy the items of your choice at a home-improvement center or a specialist store.

However, for many other items it's easier and cheaper to choose option 1: have the home delivered with the option of your choice. Let's take the electric light switches and outlets as an example. Almost certainly the home comes standard with the cheapest toggle switches and matching outlets. Retail those things are around 59¢ a piece, and there may be 12 switches in the home. (Actually, the outlets don't matter

Palm Harbor Homes photo

Fig. 14.1. With a smart and tasteful choice of interior options, like shown here for a kitchen, *your* manufactured home does not have to look like everyone else's.

much, since they're hardly visible.) In this case, option 3 is not available: You can't specify the home to be delivered without the switches and/or outlets, because it would not pass inspection that way.

Option 2 would be to have the home shipped in its standard configuration, complete with all those cheesy-looking switches. But you wanted the "Decor"type, which cost several dollars more retail, so you have them all changed out for those fancier-looking items by an electrician. After you've bought the replacement switches yourself it will still cost you an arm and a leg to hire an electrician to do that simple job. If you do it yourself (after disarming the circuit breakers), it will amaze you how many hours it will take, and how inconvenient the whole process is to the rest of the family. However, once you own a home, you will benefit greatly from learning to do jobs like that yourself.

So for things like this it's much preferable to choose option 2: Specify the upgrade to be done at the factory. Just make sure you control the process by letting them give you the list of items they're upgrading and the cost for each. The price difference should not be more than the retail cost of the items (a couple of dollars in this particular case), because there's no additional labor involved.

Outside Contractor Upgrades

For bigger jobs, especially ones that don't really affect the home's inspection and/or move-in, your best choice is Option 1: Leave the items out of the home's specification, settle for the small discount, and get what you want installed once the home is delivered.

Here is a partial list of typical items that can be handled this way:

❏ Flooring (whether carpet, sheet vinyl, hardwood, or tile)

❏ Texturing and painting (including exterior painting)

❏ Trim installation

❏ All major appliances

❏ Lighting fixtures

❏ Kitchen and bathroom fixtures

❏ Blinds, shutters, and other window coverings

15
Worksheets and Option Lists

HERE ARE some useful worksheets and lists for a manufactured home buyer (take these with you when you go shopping for one).

Land-Home Package Worksheet

Home + air conditioner + tax . . . . $_____

Land . . . . $_____

Improvements . . . . $_____

Foundation . . . . $_____

Garage . . . . $_____

Driveway, misc. concrete . . . . $_____

Septic tank . . . . $_____

Well . . . . $_____

Power . . . . $_____

City sewer and water . . . . $_____

Gas hook-up . . . . $_____

Electric . . . . $_____

Decks . . . . $_____

Permits . . . . $_____

Miscellaneous . . . . $_____

Total Project Cost . . . . $_____

Down Payment . . . . $_____

Amount to Finance . . . . $_____

Estimated taxes and insurance . . . . $_____

Total amount to finance . . . . $_____

Term of loan . . . . _____yrs.

Interest rate . . . . _____%

Monthly payment (principal and interest) $_____

Monthly taxes and insurance . . . . $_____

Monthly PMI if applicable . . . . $_____

Monthly Grand Total. . . . . $_____

Manufactured Home Community, Home-Only Worksheet

Home + air conditioner + tax . . . . $_____

City sewer and water . . . . $_____

Gas hook-up . . . . $_____

Electrical . . . . $_____

Skirting . . . . $_____

Decks, steps, fencing . . . . $_____

Permits, Miscellaneous . . . . $_____

Total Project Cost . . . . $_____

Down Payment . . . . $_____

Amount to Finance . . . . $_____

Estimated taxes and insurance . . . . $_____

Term of loan . . . . _____yrs.

Interest rate . . . . _____%

Monthly payment (principal and interest) $_____

Monthly taxes and insurance . . . . $_____

Monthly Grand Total. . . . . $_____

Essential Factory-Installed Options

Exterior

❏ At least one outside water faucet.

❏ Widest eaves possible.

❏ Super Good Cents insulation package or something comparable.

❏ Air conditioner-ready.

❏ Foundation-ready.

❏ At least 30-lb. roof load if it snows at all where you live.

Kitchen

❏ Solid wood cabinets, 12 inch minimum depth wall cabinets.

❏ Overhead light in pantry.

❏ Extra bank of drawers.

❏ Roll-out shelves or drawers for all base cabinets.

❏ Metal single-lever faucet with spray nozzle.

❏ Tile backsplash.

❏ Two fluorescent lights.

❏ Eight-inch deep sink.

❏ Metal shut-off valves under the sink.

❏ Plumbing for ice maker.

❏ Garbage disposal.

Utility Room

❏ Electric outlet for a freezer.

❏ 18-inch minimum deep cabinets over the washer and dryer.

❏ 40-gallon minimum water heater (50 or even 60-gallon is preferred if more than two people live in the house).

❏ Gas furnace, if possible.

❏ Gas water heater, if possible.

Master Bathroom

❏ Dual vitreous china wash basins.

❏ Metal faucets.

❏ Water-saving dual-flush toilet.

❏ Fiberglass or enamelled steel tub with solid-surface enclosure.

❏ 1-piece fiberglass or solid-surface shower pan and enclosure.

❏ Large mirror over wash basins with light sconces on either side.

❏ Tiled floor and walls.

❏ Metal shut-off valves under wash basin and toilet tank.

Other Bathrooms

❏ Vitreous china wash basin.

❏ Metal faucets.

❏ One-piece fiberglass tub/shower combination.

❏ Large mirror over wash basin, with sconce lights on both sides.

❏ Tile backsplash.

❏ Metal shut-off valves under wash basin and toilet tank.

❏ Water-saving dual-flush toilet.

❏ Bank of drawers.

❏ Extra storage where possible.

All Bedrooms

❏ Overhead ceiling light.

❏ Make sure windows are not in the middle of the wall.

❏ Have closets enlarged if necessary.

Living Room, Family Room, Den

❏ Additional windows to suit.

❏ Ceiling lights.

Dining Room

❏ Consider sheet vinyl or hardwood on the floor instead of carpet.

Entryway

❏ Entry sheet vinyl or tile.

Essential Options for All Rooms

❏ Check very carefully the placement of all heating registers. Make sure they don't end up in traffic patterns or where furniture should be placed. Have them moved near the exterior walls.

❏ The best carpet that is offered, or take the credit from the dealer and have your own installed. Find out the total square yards in the house, then get a price on at least a 52-ounce carpet. Simply have the dealer add the cost to the purchase price of the home.

❏ Minimum carpet pad should be 6-pound (your carpet will last much longer).

❏ Fully extending drawers with metal roller guides.

❏ Metal door knobs.

Recommended Factory Options (depending on budget)

Exterior

❏ Vinyl siding (lifetime warranty with no painting) or properly primed and painted wood or cement-fiber siding.

❏ 4:12 pitch roof (the steeper pitch looks more residential.)

❏ Recessed entry (better protection from the weather).

❏ Dormer or "peak" on the roof to eliminate the flat look.

❏ Lighter color shingles (they last longer regardless of warranty).

❏ 200-Amp electric service.

❏ French patio doors (avoid sliding glass doors).

Kitchen

❏ Upgrade appliances at least one step (more features, more durable, and more attractive).

❏ Built-in microwave-hood over the stove.

❏ Adjustable shelves.

❏ Extra bank(s) of drawers.

Utility Room

❏ Fiberglass utility sink.

❏ Gas water heater (if gas is available).

❏ 36-inch metal-clad rear door.

❏ Storage cabinets

❏ Adjustable 18-inch minimum depth shelves.

Master Bathroom

❏ Two wash basins.

❏ Bank(s) of drawers.

Other Bathrooms

❏ Bank of drawers.

Living Room, Family Room, Den

❏ Wiring for a ceiling light and/or fan.

Recommended Options for All Rooms

❏ Solid wood baseboard molding.

❏ 6-panel or solid-core doors.

❏ Tape and texture throughout.

❏ Metal single-lever door handles.

❏ Extra storage wherever possible.

❑ Ceiling light.

Factory Options to Avoid

✖ Swamp cooler on the roof (remember, holes in the roof cause leaks).

✖ Laminate flooring (it shifts during transport).

✖ Ceiling fans (instead, buy your own at a local hardware store or home-improvement center).

✖ Skylights, especially the plastic type, and even then only if the roof pitch is 4:12 minimum.

✖ Pre-installed telephone, cable TV, and Internet jacks.

✖ Storm doors.

✖ Aluminum windows (should be vinyl-clad or wood).

✖ Towel bars and tissue holders (buy your own of better quality).

✖ Curtains (buy your own floor-to-ceiling curtains).

✖ ³/₈ inch drywall (should be ½ inch minimum).

✖ Outswing exterior doors (should be inswing).

✖ 2 x 4 exterior walls (should be 2 x 6).

✖ Interior walls less than 2 x 4.

✖ Plastic light covers (glass only, please).

✖ Log siding, cedar siding, or metal siding (choose either vinyl or painted wood).

✖ Wood-burning stoves, pellet stoves, or fireplaces (buy your own of higher quality).

16
Flow Sheets

O N THE FOLLOWING pages, you will find systematic listings of the order of events in the process of buying a manufactured home. In the first section, we'll look at the process involved when the home is to be placed on your own land, based on a typical case. The second part will deal with the process of placing the home in a manufactured home community.

Home-Land Package Flow Sheet

1. Go to a bank, credit union, or mortgage company. Go through the loan approval process, so you know exactly how much money you can borrow. It can take up to two weeks. Do this *before* you go shopping for a home.

2. While waiting for approval, begin to gather bids on the site improvements from contractors that come highly recommended.

3. When you have been notified of an approval, go shopping for a home and take the purchase agreement for the home, the purchase agreement for the land, and all the bids for the improvements to the lender.

4. The lender will then order an appraisal. Be prepared to part with somewhere around $500. The appraisal can take 1 to 3 weeks.

5. During this time, check on building permits at the court house. These folks will give you specific instructions regarding what paperwork they need from you and will generally work with you.

6. When the appraisal comes back and is satisfactory to the lender, take a copy of the approval letter to the home dealer and have him order the home.

7. Next, call the contractors and have them start the improvements on your land. Please note: Depending on the program you have qualified for at your lender, and depending on the seller of the land, you may have to close on the land before the seller will allow improvements to start.

8. Stay in close contact with your contractors. As each one completes his respective job, the local building inspector will sign off on that improvement. When the foundation is complete, notify the dealer and have the home delivered.

9. Hopefully, the dealer won't take more than 7 to 10 working days to install and finish the home. When all the improvements are complete and the detail work on the home is done, the lender will order a final inspection by the appraiser.

10. Upon completion of the final inspection, a closing date at a title company will be set. This is when you will have to bring any funds in and when you officially become the homeowner.

11. The title company will then send payment to the manufactured home dealer, the contractors, and anyone else to whom funds are due.

This is just a typical scenario. Your particular transaction may differ in some areas. This is not science, but rather an art. A land-home package can take 90 days or more.

Home-Only Flow Sheet

Here is a systematic listing of the steps you have to take when buying only the home, without buying land and worrying about the many improvements required.

1. Go to a bank or mortgage broker and go through the loan approval process. It can take up to two weeks. This way you will know exactly how much money you can borrow. Do this *before* you go shopping for a home. If you decide to finance at a dealer, ask to see the approval letter to check that the dealer did not "bump up" the interest rate.

2. Once you have loan approval, you can begin shopping for a home.

3. When you find a home and settle on a price, you can have the dealer add the cost of things like an awning, a deck, or skirting to the cost of the home. This is what you will take back to the mortgage company.

   Note: Some dealers will offer to line up skirting and decking, etc. This is fine; however, some dealers will charge more than these improvements actually cost—it is pure profit for them. Take some extra time and get independent bids. You will probably save some money. Our recommendation is that, when you get a price on the home, you request a "delivered and set" price only. You can then shop around yourself for improvements. It is easy enough to find contractors for skirting and any others jobs needed on the internet, and call them to get their bids. Get all bids in writing. Take them to the dealership and have those costs added to the purchase agreement.

4. If you are going to place your home in a manufactured home community, get an application from the one of your choice. The management will have to contact the dealer for pertinent information, such as home size, utility locations, and so on.

5. The mortgage company will need copies of the purchase agreement on the home and of the lease agreement from the community.

6. Some dealers will require 5 to 10 % down before delivery of the home. Make sure you know up-front.

7. The community manager and the dealer will agree on a time for delivery of your home, and for the decks, skirting, and any other improvement that needs to be done. You also need to follow up on this to make sure communication is adequate.

6. Upon final inspection, you will sign closing papers at a title company and they will send the moneys due the dealer and all other parties involved.

This too is a typical scenario. Your particular transaction may go differently in some details, but these are the most important steps involved and their typical sequence. A home-only purchase can take 20 to 45 days.

Fig. 16.1. Cute as a bug. This is an exterior view of the same home of which the floor plan is shown on page 41, finished and ready for move-in— assuming everything covered in this chapter has been taken care of.

17

Warranties

WHAT TYPE of warranty do you have and for how long? In this chapter, you'll find a listing of all the items that should be covered. Carefully read the contract your dealer is offering you and compare it with this chart to make sure everything is covered—and if not, negotiate for it.

Manufacturer should warranty the following:

At least one year for:

1. Plumbing fixtures (toilets, sinks, shower stalls, bathtubs, faucets).

2. Light fixtures (porch lights, ceiling and wall-mount lights, outlets, switches, and circuit breakers).

3. Appliances provided by the manufacturer (refrigerator, stove, cook top, garbage disposal, range, microwave, trash compactor, dishwasher, furnace, water heater, washer, dryer).

4. Cosmetic defects (scratches on walls, ceilings, doors, cabinets, moldings, counter tops, appliances, plumbing fixtures; stained or damaged window coverings; cracked or broken electrical cover plates; stained or damaged shower door; torn shower curtains; damaged hardware, such as door knobs, pulls, etc.; tile or trim

caulking defects; stained or damaged siding, trim, or shutters; torn or damaged screens).

5. Fans (bath and kitchen exhaust fans and ceiling fans).

6. Roof structure (roof rafters, main support beam, insulation, wood roof decline, all support lumber contained within roof).

At least 5 years for:

7. Exterior and interior walls and ceilings (studs, insulation, framing members, all support lumber contained within the outside and inside walls, ceiling surface materials).

8. Electrical system (wiring, fittings, connections, fixture boxes, junction boxes, main and sub-panel boxes).

9. Plumbing system (water pipes, drain pipes, gas and oil pipes, fittings, pipe connections, fixture and appliance connections).

10. Frame or chassis (tow bar, steel structure beneath floor of home).

The following must be in writing on the purchase agreement:

Dealer is to warranty:

1. Set-up of home according to manufacturer's specifications.

2. Service hook-ups (if done by dealer).

3. Anything else customer and dealer put in writing.

The dealer does have a "shared" responsibility with the manufacturer but may state in the agreement something like "dealer provides no express or implied warranty." Simply put, it completely releases the dealer from liability should your home be a "lemon." But don't get alarmed: this is typical. It's very similar to buying a new car: the dealer is not responsible for the warranty of the car, *but the manufacturer is*. If you have work done on your vehicle under warranty, the dealer in turn bills the manufacturer for parts and labor. It's the same with manufactured homes.

A dependable, responsible dealer will have his own service department and should be able to attend to any service needs that may arise.

My suggestion for the quickest service is to first call the dealer. If they can't get to you in 10 days or less, call the factory service department. They may be able to take care of it more quickly.

All the appliances in your home have their own factory warranty. If your refrigerator were to break down, the dealer would call someone in the area who is authorized to work on your brand of appliance. Personally, we'd get the name and number from the dealer and call ourselves, because that's much quicker.

Warranties on siding, roof shingles, carpet, and windows are handled in a similar manner.

Be as thorough as you can when it comes to spelling out who is responsible for warranty work. Dealers and manufacturers are quite notorious for quibling over who is responsible for what—while you are waiting in the middle. Spell it out and don't be hesitant to call the manufacturer if the dealer does not respond to your satisfaction.

Something you may want to try is to hold back a certain amount of money from the dealer, say 10–20%. This way, you can inspect the house and determine that it is completed to your satisfaction, and then you release the rest of the money to the dealer. Some dealers will flat-out refuse this, but it can't hurt to try. If you can't get satisfaction from either party, there are State Administrative Agencies, whose address for your state can be found on the Web.

Check List

Once your home is set up and finished, your dealer should do a thorough walk-through with you for a sort of "how-to" session and to make sure all finish work is complete. They should have a checklist that you can use for service needs. Before you move any furniture in, use the list on the following three pages to check for yourself that the home was completed to your satisfaction.

If anything is missing, damaged, or improperly installed, take it up in writing and in person with the dealer right away. Provide him with a copy of your checklist, and highlight the item under contention.

	Exterior	
1.	Are all shingles on the roof accounted for?	
2.	Is the marriage line of the home sealed with a trim board and painted correctly?	
3.	Does the bottom trim on the house cover where the foundation meets the bottom of the home?	
4.	Are there any cracks, chips, or dings in the siding?	
5.	Is there a vent "flapper" covering the vent for the dryer?	
6.	Do the front and rear entry doors open, close, and lock smoothly?	
7.	Is there a black vapor barrier under the house?	
8.	Is the skirting secure and of the right color?	
9.	Are there metal straps wrapped around the I-beams and secured to an anchor bolt, either in the foundation footing or, if a park-set, then to an anchor bolt that is driven into the ground? Straps and anchor bolts should be placed every 10 to 12 feet, depending on code and manufacturer's requirements.	
10.	Make sure that the heat duct cross-over is not touching the ground and has no kinks or bends in it.	
11.	Make sure that the "belly paper" that holds the insulation under the home is tear-free.	
	Kitchen	
1.	Place a ball on the counter tops. Does it stay in place?	
2.	Are all the cabinet doors straight?	
3.	Did you get the right appliances?	
4.	Check for cuts in the sheet vinyl	
5.	Check water pressure at all faucets	
6	Do the drawers roll smoothly?	

Master Bathroom

1.	Are the wash basins and tub and shower stall scratch-free?	
2.	Does the shower door open and close so it seals properly?	
3.	Check sheet vinyl for cuts	
4.	Do the drawers roll smoothly?	
5.	Are the cabinet doors straight?	

Other Bathrooms

1.	Are the wash basin and tub scratch-free?	
2.	Check sheet vinyl if applicable	
3.	Check drawers and cabinet doors	

Bedrooms

1.	If you specified different locations for the windows, are they in the right location?	

Living Room, Dining Room, Family Room, Den

1.	Did you get those extra windows you ordered?	

Utility Room

1.	Check sheet vinyl for cuts	

Electrical

1.	Did the ceiling get the wiring for a ceiling light and/or fan?	

Tape and Texture

1.	Check the entire ceiling and walls, including the inside of the closets, for even texture application and that there are no bulges in the drywall. You should not see any drywall seams.	

All Rooms		
1.	Are all the outlets and light switches straight?	
2.	Are the heat vents in the right places?	
3.	Do all the interior doors open properly; do they close smoothly and lock correctly?	
4.	Do all the windows open and close smoothly and latch correctly?	
5.	Is the carpet or sheet vinyl free from "waves" or "bubbles"?	
6.	Has the baseboard been installed?	
7.	Are the doors and trim free from gouges and other damage?	
8.	Is the marriage line of the home, where the sections join, even?	
9.	Are all mini blinds installed and do they function properly?	
10.	Do all the interior door moldings meet properly in the corners with a minimum amount of patching compound or caulking?	
11.	Do all the doors that are supposed to have locking knobs have them?	

You will have to use the option sheet with which the home was ordered and the standard features list to make sure everything you ordered is in the home when it is delivered.

The home will come with a thick package of information, covering subjects ranging from warranty to maintenance and operation. Read it all very thoroughly. It will save you time when it comes to operating things properly and fixing them in case of minor problems.

General Maintenance Tips

The following list summarizes the types of maintenance work you should do, or have done, on various components of your manufactured home on a regular basis:

Hardboard siding	This product will have to be painted every three to five years, depending on the quality of paint, its application, and the weather conditions. It needs to be sealed at all times to prevent water damage. Make sure to put polyurethane caulking over door and window trim. It is easy to put vinyl siding over hardboard if you get tired of repainting.
Fixing squeaking floors	Have a helper stand over the squeaking portion, rocking back and forth, making it easy to find its exact location as you crawl under the house. Find the loose outrigger that extends from the I-beam, and tighten the bolts snugly.
Tape and texture	If you have a home with wallpaper over drywall, it is possible to apply tape and texture over it. Check with a local contractor for best results. Keep in mind that if you replace all the drywall in preparation to tape and texture, the new drywall should be $5/8$ in., as opposed to the original $3/8$ in. This means you will also have to replace trim around the windows and doors.
Appliances, fixtures, etc.	Follow the specific manufacturer's directions for taking care of appliances, bathroom and kitchen fixtures, floor covering, etc.

18
More About Contracts

FOR YOUR PROTECTION, please make sure the home dealer puts the following wording in your contract to purchase:

1. Deposits given to dealer by customer are 100 % refundable anytime except after home is ordered.

2. Price is guaranteed for 120 days.

3. Purchase of home is contingent upon financing.

4. Dealer will facilitate warranty between customer and factory.

5. Dealer will re-level home within one year of delivery.

6. Dealer will provide free tape and texture repair within one year of delivery.

7. Customer retains the right to choose the contractor and any sub-contractor to complete any phase of home set-up including, but not limited to, transport, set-up of home, and/or finish work, tape and texture, carpet installation, and cleaning.

It is important to include all these items, especially the last one. It gives you the right to choose any contractor you want to set up your home. But make sure the people you choose to do any phase are licensed and know what they are doing. Don't hire your uncle because he will do something cheaper for you but doesn't know what he is doing.

How to Be in Control When You Shop

Now you can go shopping for your home. You will encounter sales-people and dealers who do not care about you and only want one thing—your money. Use the following steps and you will save money. You may or may not have an idea of what brand or floor plan or even what these pretty manufactured homes cost, so stick with this program.

1. Since you have done a land/home worksheet and have been qualified at a bank or some other financial institution, you know right where you stand. Do not give any of this information to a salesperson.

2. You need to see several homes, so tell the salesperson you wish to see 2-, 3-, or 4-bedroom homes—whichever you are in the market for—and you need prices on all of them. If you are asked what kind of payment or what price range you're looking for, say that you haven't gotten that far yet. *Don't go to a salesperson's office at this stage.*

3. Take note of all the houses you are interested in, get floor plans and prices and be on your way. Do not give any information to the salesman or dealer except your first name. Make sure you have all the standard features for each model.

4. Take your time at several dealerships, and look at multiple brands and floor plans, and take copious notes. Be polite, but tough. Be sure to take a copy of our "Materials" check list along.

5. When you have made a decision on a brand and a model, the fun begins. Go to the dealership and "spec" out the house you are interested in. Take copies of the "Options" worksheet pages with you, and start checking off items. Have the salesperson give you a "delivered-and-set" base price to your site. Then ask for a copy of the options sheet and the base price in writing. Tell the salesperson you need to go home and go over your paperwork. If they won't part with it, say good-bye and walk out.

6. More than likely there is another dealership selling the same products somewhere nearby. Simply walk through the same scenario. You may have to do this two or three times before you get what you want.

7. Do not let the salesman write on *your* spec sheet. Have him do his own for you.

8. Never tell a dealer what you were quoted elsewhere for the house you are negotiating for.

This last point bears some explaining. Harvey Mackay does that in his book *Swim with the Sharks Without Being Eaten Alive*, in a chapter titled "Calling Mr. Otis."

It's a sales scam very common in the car business. It goes something like this: You have gone to different dealers and negotiated all day, all month. You've finally made a deal, and the salesperson writes it up. He casually asks you what price the other dealers were asking. At this point, flushed with victory, you throw away the most valuable asset you have—information (the other dealers' prices).

"Just one last step," the salesperson says, "the sales manager has to okay the deal." He gets on the intercom and says, "Calling Mr. Otis."

Of course, there is no Mr. Otis. He may be the sales manager, but his name is something else. The sales manager shows up and pulls the salesperson out of the room to let you, the prospect stew a while. The salesperson finally comes back, saying, "Otis won't go for the deal, and then proceeds to "retrace" it up to exactly the same price you told him the other dealers were asking.

Because you now have too much invested emotionally, and your kids are jumping around, you think, "If I don't take this deal, I'll have to start all over again."

So what's $5,000 more on a $80,000 house? Just a few more monthly payments? At a five percent interest rate, that's $26.80 more per month, or nearly $10,000 more in payments over the life of your 30-year mortgage. Don't fall for the Mr. Otis trick.

The Price to Pay

The choice of which home is right for you is a personal one. You have the list of base prices, the list of materials, and the formula for figuring out the approximate cost that the dealer paid the factory for the home. Your budget will give you some direction, and which dealer you felt the best about comes into play as well.

So how do you deal for the best price? Some dealers will part with a home at cost, but most will not. It is your job to find the least amount of profit a dealer will take. Start with an offer of the price you have figured and wait for a reaction. The dealer will come back with a price, and then the negotiation begins. Play the game. Go back and forth a few times. Never raise your price more than $200 at a time. If you are dissatisfied, begin to get up and leave. You may or may not be given the deal you want, but that's why there are other dealers. Don't be pressured with, "If I can get the price you want, will you buy today?" Tell them you don't know.

Once a price has been agreed upon, the salesman will ask for a deposit, usually 5 to 10 % down. Give him only $100 and tell him he'll get an approval letter from your bank. Make sure the contract has the clauses in it that we have spelled out at the beginning of this chapter.

Also, once you have a base price for the home you want, ask the dealer for the name and phone number of the contractor who will be responsible for setting up your home. Call them to get their contractor's license number, and ask what they charge, based on where your property is located and whether the home will be set on a foundation. You'll also have to tell the contractor the size of the home and whether it is a single-, double-, or triple-wide.

Next, ask for the name of the contractor who will do the tape and texture close-up on the home. Call and tell them where the home will be and the dimensions. Get their estimate.

Now it is time to ask who will install the carpet. Call the carpet dealer with the number of square yards in the house and get an estimate. Remember: no factory carpet.

If you are going to set your home on blocks and not on a foundation, you will need some type of skirting. Vinyl is the most popular. Call to get an estimate. Again, the contractor will need to know the size of the house and where it will be installed.

Tell the dealer you will clean the home yourself once all phases are done. Tell them you want a check made out to you for $200. Alternately, you could reduce the price you pay for the house by $200 instead.

If you are trying to determine the exact dealer set-up cost of the home, and the dealer refuses to tell you which contractors they use to complete your home, you will have to search on-line and get your own bids. It's up to you to find reputable people yourself. Ask for references, and take all steps to find out if these contractors do good work. If you find someone to do a set-up phase for your home that the dealer doesn't use, tell the dealer who you do want to use and have the dealer and the contractor get together so they can begin scheduling.

You can even call the freight company who will deliver your house and get an estimate.

Take down all these estimates and add them together. Take the total and deduct it from the base price of the house. This process involves a lot of work, but it can save you thousands. Dealers often add to each of these costs for a little extra profit, but there's no need for you to pay more than the actual costs.

Doing all this yourself is time-consuming, but it will give you the real costs of setting up your home. This is a powerful tool in negotiation. Use it.

Because you are getting the home you want, with the proper options, equipped the way you want it to be, don't be surprised at the final cost. Even though you've followed our guidelines and come to an agreement with a dealer, your cost for a 1,700 to 2,000 square foot home could be $150,000 or more once installed. But look at the comparative figures for the total cost estimates in the following table:

Feature	Manufactured Home (1,700 sq. ft.)	Site-built home (1,500 sq. ft.)
Home	$95,000–$125,000	$240,000–$320,000
Land	$25,000–$35,000 (100 x 100 ft. lot)	included (80 x 100 ft. lot)
2-car garage	$18,000–$24,000	included
Foundation	$4,000–$7,000	included
Septic tank	$2,500–$4,000	included
Power	$1,500–$2,000	included
Permits	$2,000–$3,000	included
Total	$148,000–$200,000	$240,000–320,000

These numbers tell a huge story: Manufactured homes still give you the opportunity to own more square feet, more land, and give you a bigger range of total cost—depending on where you live and the deal you make on the house. Ask yourself these questions:

❏ Is the home big enough?

❏ Is it located on a large enough lot?

❏ Is it energy-efficient and built to your satisfaction?

Look at the difference in total finished cost per square foot (including land and improvements).

Manufactured home . . . . $88–$117

Site-built home . . . . $160–$210

Your costs could even be lower if you educate yourself and learn that it is OK to negotiate with everyone, including landowners, contractors, and, of course, dealers. You must take charge of the whole process.

Today's manufactured homes are incredibly energy-efficient and offer hundreds of floor plans, options and details. Don't let the size of the project intimidate you. You will save money and get a great house.

Quick Materials Checklist

1.	How is this house built and with what materials?	
2.	Are shingles 20-, 25-, or 30-year warranty?	
3.	Are they held down with nails or staples?	
4.	How many nails per shingle?	
5.	Is felt used on the roof decking?	
6.	What size are the roof trusses (2 x 2, 2 x 3, 2 x 4)?	
7.	How far apart are they?	
8.	How is the attic cavity vented?	
9.	Are the windows continuous-weld and vinyl-clad?	
10.	Is the siding 20-, 25-, or 30-year or lifetime warranted?	
11.	If vinyl siding, is it attached to a ⅜-inch backer boards?	

12.	Does the home come with Tyvek house wrap?	
13.	What type of paint, and how many coats, is used on the exterior?	
14.	What are the R-values of the insulation? Ceiling Wall Floor	
15.	What size are the floor joists (2 x 6, 2 x 8)?	
16.	Do the floor joists run with the floor deck or across it (longitudinal or transverse)?	
17.	How thick is the floor decking and what material is it made of?	
18.	How thick is the drywall—½ inch, or ⅜ inch?	
19.	How is the drywall fastened to the studs?	
20.	Are the window sills wood, taped and textured, or vinyl-wrapped?	
21.	Are the mini blinds metal or plastic?	
22.	What is the standard carpet pad? (should be 6- or 7-pound minimum)	
23.	Are the hinges on the door mortised?	
24.	What are the interior doors made of?	
25.	Are the doorknobs metal or plastic?	
26.	Are the cabinets solid wood?	
27.	How many drawers are there?	

Glossary of Terms

ACV	Actual cash value, a term used to describe what a dealer would sell your trade-in for to a wholesaler.
APR	Annual Percentage Rate, the actual interest rate payable on the outstanding balance of a home mortgage.
ARM	Adjustable Rate Mortgage, a loan with an interest rate that goes up and/or down over time.
"Be-backs"	Customers who tell salespeople they'll be back.
"Bird dogs"	People who refer potential home buyers to salespeople for money.
"Bumping"	Getting a potential customer to raise his offer on a home
Close	When the home buyer is talked into signing a purchase agreement.
"Closer"	An employee of the dealership whose only job is to get customers to sign purchase agreements.
Display model	A home which a dealer will display as a model home and then sell in a few months at a "reduced price."
Equity	The value in a home when the payoff is subtracted from the total amount to finance.
Finance charge	The total charges when a customer finances a home, including interest, fees, and other charges.
Floor planning, or Flooring	When the homes at a dealership are owned by financing institutions rather than the dealer.
Gross back end	Profit a dealer makes on financing and insurance.
Gross front end	Profit a dealer makes on the sale of a home.
Hard money	Same as ACV.
Kickback, Holdback, VIP money	Profit built into each home invoice. It is a percentage of the invoice and is paid to the dealer once a year. This should be *your* money.
PAC	The cost a dealer pays to have a home delivered and set up. Extra profit is sometimes added here.
Payment buyers	Customers who are concerned only about their monthly payment, not about the bottom-line price.

"Skating"	When a salesperson does business with another salesperson's customer.
"Spiffs"	Cash bonuses paid to salespeople for selling a certain model home or achieving a certain number of "write-ups."
"T.O."	To turn over a customer to another sales person, sales manager, or closer.
"Ups"	Walk-in customers. Salespeople take turns taking "ups" by watching the front door.
Upside down	If you trade in your home and find out that you owe more than the house is worth.
"Write-up"	Signed purchase agreement.

* Phrases in quotation marks are unofficial trade jargon; phrases not so marked are dictionary-defined terms.

Right: Fig. 19.1. An interesting high-end manufactured home, with all the qualities and charm of a site-built home—at a 25% savings.

Below: Fig. 19.2. This humble single-wide is perfect for a weekend or vacation retreat.

MHI photo

Palm Harbor Homes image

Index